SOUL SEARCH

ROBERT S. RICKER
with Ron Pitkin

Regal Books

A Division of GL Publications
Ventura, California, U.S.A.

Other good reading in this series:

Profiles in Faith (Old Testament Personalities)
   by William D. Mounce
Bound for Joy (Philippians)
   by Stuart Briscoe
Confronted by Love (2 Corinthians)
   by Dan Baumann
God with Us (Matthew)
   by D. A. Carson

Published by Regal Books
A Division of GL Publications
Ventura, California 93006
Printed in U.S.A.

Unless otherwise noted, the Bible text in this publication is from the Holy Bible: *The New International Version.* Copyright © 1978 by The International Bible Society. Used by permission of Zondervan Bible Publishers.

Other versions quoted include:
KJV, King James Version
RSV, Revised Standard Version of the Bible, copyrighted 1946 and 1952 by the Division of Christian Education of the NCCC, U.S.A., and used by permission.
Phillips, The New Testament in Modern English, Revised Edition, J.B. Phillips, Translator. © J. B. Phillips 1958, 1960, 1972. Used by permission of MacMillan Publishing Co., Inc.
TLB, from *The Living Bible,* Copyright © 1971 by Tyndale House Publishers, Wheaton, Illinois. Used by permission.
TEV, from *Good News Bible,* the Bible in Today's English version. Old Testament copyright © American Bible Society, 1976. New Testament copyright © American Bible Society, 1966, 1971, 1976. Used by permission.

Library of Congress Cataloging in Publication Data.

Ricker, Robert S., 1938-
   Soulsearch: hope for 21st century living from Ecclesiastes.

   (A Bible commentary for laymen)
    1. Bible. O.T. Ecclesiastes—Commentaries.
I. Pitkin, Ronald E., 1942-   . II. Title.
II. Series.
BS1475.3.R55   1985   223'.807   85-21594
ISBN 0-8307-1100-7

  4 5 6 7 8 9 10 11 12 / 91 90 89 88

Rights for publishing this book in other languages are contracted by Gospel Literature International (GLINT) foundation. GLINT also provides technical help for the adaptation, translation, and publishing of Bible study resources and books in scores of languages worldwide. For further information, contact GLINT, Post Office Box 488, Rosemead, California, 91770, U.S.A., or the publisher.

To my wife, Dee,
who has made Ecclesiastes 9:9 easy and fun,
and to our children, Todd and Kristen,
who have brought us unspeakable joy
and in truth are
"a heritage from the Lord"
(Ps. 127:3).

Contents

For adult classes wishing to study this book, a
coursebook with teacher's materials and reproducible
in-class student pages is available from your church
supplier.

ACKNOWLEDGMENTS

Long before I ever thought about studying the book of Ecclesiastes, I had learned a great deal about its truths. My mother and father had taught them to me, largely in the course of daily life.

All during my growing-up years, I sat under my father's powerful preaching, hoping that some day God would be able to use me as He was using him. He challenged me to live for God and for eternal realities. My precious mother, a real Bible student and gifted communicator in her own right, also gave me her rich insight into life and pastoring.

I will never forget the day when she told her young preacher-son, "Bob, if you teach the Scriptures well to your congregation and let them know you love them, they'll overlook many weaknesses."

So, thanks, Mother and Dad. You taught me where to find lasting happiness in life, and I love you for it. When God chose parents for me, He picked out the very best. And I'm so grateful, to Him and to you.

A few years ago I preached through Ecclesiastes at Grace Church Edina in Minnesota. These dear people responded to the great and timeless themes of Ecclesiastes with enthusiasm. One man had even come to me one day to say, "You can stay in

Ecclesiastes as long as you like!" Furthermore, I knew it was a book many can hardly *find* in the Bible, much less understand. Having just finished months of study on it, I knew how contemporary and relevant it was. It is a book come of age.

I was encouraged to write a book based on my study. But with my busy schedule, I knew I did not have time to write a book. However, the Lord soon provided another man who has been fascinated with Ecclesiastes for many years. Before long, Ron Pitkin and I were busy writing and rewriting, traveling and corresponding between Nashville and Minneapolis.

So, many thanks to you, Ron, for the excellent job you did in taking the rough, verbal form and turning it into a readable, thoughtful manuscript. You have become more than a co-author and editor. You have become a good friend. Without your hard work, the book would not have been written. Working with you has been a blessing.

BOB RICKER

INTRODUCTION

Ecclesiastes: A Book Whose Time Has Come

I normally look at a map before venturing on a journey.

Several years ago, my family and I drove from Arizona to our home in Minnesota. Having misplaced my road atlas, I drove the entire way by memory. I probably should have purchased a new atlas, but I had decided to try the trip without one. In spite of a few missed turns, eventually I made it back safely. But my trip would have been much easier if I had taken the time and money necessary to buy a map.

I approach the reading of a book with that same road-map philosophy. I first turn to the introduction or first chapter, for usually a good book will give me a reliable "road map" in one of those places. It charts out the terrain over which the author wishes to take me; it expounds the benefits I will enjoy from reading it; it defines the questions it will ask and answer. In short, it tells me what to expect.

So I have prepared this introductory chapter with these questions in mind: What is this book and why should I read it? How will it help me make sense out of the book of Ecclesiastes? And how will it help me make sense out of life?

Of Life and Wisdom

The book of Ecclesiastes is a book about life. Its writer, King Solomon, was a realist.[1] In fact, I would even call him a realist's realist! He writes with candor about frustration, fulfillment, work, sex, injustice, friendship, worship, happiness, insecurity, suffering, temptation, folly, confusion, emptiness—our concerns. Even more importantly, he writes about these topics with a kind of brutal honesty and unsentimental clarity that even today few would dare to express in a religious book. His observations are really the conclusions that life itself forces upon us— if we have the stomach for the truth.

Ecclesiastes is also a book about wisdom. Solomon writes that we need two kinds of wisdom. The first is the wisdom that tells us how to get things done in this world—*practical wisdom*. If you want to get ahead in life and want to avoid trouble, Ecclesiastes has some sound practical advice. How do things work? How can I get the most out of life? Ecclesiastes will tell you.

The second type of wisdom is God's wisdom. This *spiritual wisdom* tells us what is eternally important. True, it is wise not to whisper sedition against the king (see 10:20); it is also wise to know that God made us (see 12:1) and that He will eventually pass judgment on our lives (see 12:14). That is, it is one thing to fear the king; it is quite another to fear God. It is this kind of wisdom Solomon had in mind when he wrote, "The fear of the Lord is the beginning of wisdom" (Prov. 9:10).

Is That All There Is?

Do you ever get blue watching the evening news? I confess I do. In our city, like yours, crime is increasing. The legitimate poor are struggling because of new regulations brought on by welfare cheaters. A new abortion clinic is opening. The gays want rights, not repentance. I go to the monthly ministerial meeting looking for an encouraging note. It's not there. One church is going through a split. Another evangelical pastor has left his wife. Lord, what do you have to tell us?

Solomon constructs an interesting answer in Ecclesiastes. Simply put, he says that all human striving is worthless. It is not worth the puff of wind it takes to blow it away. In writing these rather strong words, "Utterly meaningless! Everything is meaningless" (1:2), I believe King Solomon had his eye on two people. First, he was looking back on his own life with remorse over his follies. Second, he was looking at the all-too-common pagan (today we call him a "secularist") who sees no reason to involve God in his life. "I do quite well without God's help, thank you." Quite successful in his own eyes, he looks down at those who believe God is important.

So Solomon decides to meet the secular person on his own ground. It is as though he says, "OK. Let's assume that God is irrelevant. But if God is out of the picture, who's in? What does life become without Him?"

The first element he finds is *death.* Death is a rather serious problem for the person who has all his or her eggs in an earthly basket. Death is a fact of life that cannot be avoided. "Like the fool, the wise man too must die" (2:16). For all we can see, that might as well be life's final verdict.

The second element Solomon finds is *evil.* He finds evil everywhere. Wickedness where justice should be executed (see 3:16), oppression of the poor in favor of the powerful (see 4:1), envy that accompanies every success (see 4:4), the greed of the wealthy (see 4:8), social systems that exploit (see 5:8), sinful people everywhere (see 7:20), and a mad thirst for evil (see 9:3)—all fill the earth. These evils, too, are easy to observe.

The third fact Solomon finds is *time and chance* (see 9:11,12). He explodes the myth that people can master their own fate. Instead, time and chance end up getting all of us. We are like the unsuspecting fish that is rudely taken from the water when his time "falls unexpectedly" upon him (see 9:12). All of us have seen the brutal work of time and chance; we see their effects every day.

So this is what life without God is like. And having made his point, Solomon again declares, "Meaningless! Meaningless! . . . Everything is meaningless!" (12:8). Thus Solomon both begins and ends his description of life with these bookends of despair.

No, There's More

But Solomon is a man of faith, and he is not willing to leave the reader in that bone-chilling condition. He cannot resist proclaiming his own faith as he rests his case:

> Now all has been heard; here is the conclusion of the
> matter: Fear God and keep his commandments, for
> this is the whole duty of man. For God will bring every
> deed into judgment, including every hidden thing,
> whether it is good or evil (12:13,14).

Even though Ecclesiastes is filled with statements about the futility of the human experience, Solomon is too much a man of faith to hide his own beliefs. He has much to say about God, even though he uses few words to say it.

In the course of Ecclesiastes he uses five separate attributes of God to express his convictions.

1. As *Creator,* God makes all things. We are told that we "cannot understand the work of God, the Maker of all things" (11:5). It is He who creates, not us; and we cannot change it. Everything has its season (see 3:1-8), and not one of us can do so much as make a crooked thing straight (see 7:13) or make the wind blow one way or another (see 11:5).

2. As *Sovereign,* God is in charge. It is God who has given a "heavy burden" to humanity (1:13); it is God who "gives wisdom, knowledge and happiness" to the one "who pleases him," but takes the sinners' work from them (2:26); and it is God who protects "the righteous and the wise and what they do" (9:1).

3. As *Wisdom,* God is unsearchable. In 3:11 we are told "He also has set eternity in the hearts of men; yet they cannot fathom what God has done from beginning to end." In 7:14 we are also told that God has made good and bad times and "therefore, a man cannot discover anything about his future." Furthermore, even a wise person will be unable to understand the works of God (see 7:23,24; 8:17).

4. As the *Righteous One,* God will surely judge. He will judge the wicked (see 3:17); the works of the righteous are in

His hand (see 9:1); we are to live with the judgment in mind, even from the days of our youth (see 11:9); and ultimately everything and everyone will experience God's judgment (see 12:14).

5. As *Love,* God can be trusted. I believe this is what Solomon implied when he wrote: "So I reflected on all this and concluded that the righteous and the wise and what they do are in God's hands, but no man knows whether love or hate awaits him" (9:1).

I do not believe that Solomon is saying that we cannot know whether God is a God of love. It is important to remember that, by inspiration of God, he is presenting his argument to the secular-minded person. It seems to me that what he says is, "OK, for the sake of argument, this time let's assume there is a God. But based on what we see around us—evil and suffering and death—we really can't tell whether He loves or hates us. So what is the point of talking about it?"

Of course Solomon knew that God loves us! He knew the answer to his question. For those who do not know the answer, however, it is a terrifying question. But all who know Solomon's God also know that it is a wonderful question. "Ah, yes! He loves me. That's the kind of God He is."

A Faith-Filled Perspective

It would be easy to assume that a book filled with "vanity of vanities" (1:2, *KJV*) would advocate a pinch-faced approach to life. But that is not the case. Repeatedly, Solomon declares that life is a gift from God, and we are to live it with joy (see 2:24,25; 3:13; 5:18-20; 8:15; 9:7-9; 11:9). Certainly, in view of his keen awareness of the dark side of life, his is a remarkable, faith-filled perspective. We who are blessed with so much would do well to learn of joy and gratitude from him.

As I study the book of Ecclesiastes, I find it to be a practical and reliable guide to twentieth-century life. Time and again I have been amazed at how accurately Solomon described the world. It never fails to overwhelm me that in spite of its surface cynicism, the message of Ecclesiastes is as reliable and hope-filled in our modern, secular age as it was when first penned thousands of years ago. That is why I love this book.

Come, walk through it with me.

NOTE

1. The authors realize that some commentators believe Ecclesiastes was written by someone other than Solomon. However, we have accepted the historic understanding of the book's authorship as Solomon, partly due to its similarity in expression and phraseology with the Song of Solomon, partly due to the weight of scholarly opinion, and partly because it is hard to make sense of the book if Solomon was not its author including 1:1.

CHAPTER ONE

Why Does My Life
Seem So Pointless?

Ecclesiastes 1:1-11

He was a brilliant man. Those who knew him well and those who only knew him by reputation said he had more than just raw intelligence. He was able to *use* what he knew. He was wise.

And yet, as I read his story, I thought of how incredibly foolish he had been. Born into wealth and power, he had been raised with all the advantages they offer. He had enjoyed the best education money could buy. Loved by his father, King David, he was handpicked to be his successor.

As he followed in his father's steps, success followed upon success. His accomplishments even outdid his father's. It was not long, however, before he slipped into an all-too-familiar pattern. He became involved with one new woman, then another. Then many. Soon he abandoned the principles by which both he and his father had expanded their holdings. He became harsh and arbitrary in his decisions. He drifted away from God and the principles he had been taught as a child.

He simply lost his way.

As I continued to follow his story, I learned that eventually he returned to those basic convictions of his youth. He saw how foolish a wise man can be when he takes his eyes off God. So he repented of his foolishness and his sin. And his willingness to turn from dissolute pleasure-seeking to serving God and humanity caused his reputation as a wise man to spread far and wide.

His name? King Solomon of Israel.

I believe it was sometime late in his life—perhaps as he sat reflecting on the folly of his younger years—that he resolved to use his God-given insight and intelligence to show us all how life really is and how to better navigate through it.

Not life as the image-makers and manipulators want us to see it, mind you. Not life as the users and exploiters want us to view it. Not life as those who have a stake in our not thinking clearly want us to feel about it.

No. Solomon wanted to paint a picture of the truth that all could see, in his day and in ours. He wanted everyone to know exactly what life holds for the person who has no use for God, or who talks as if he does but ignores Him. He also wanted everyone to know exactly what life will be like for those who love the Lord, learn justice and mercy, and walk humbly before God. No sentiment. No punches pulled. Just the truth.

So he wrote a book. We call it the book of Ecclesiastes, which is its title in the Greek version of the Old Testament. In Hebrew the title is *Quoheleth,* which can mean either one who collects wise sayings or one who speaks to an assembly—"The Preacher," as many versions translate it. The *New International Version* translates it as "The Teacher," which expresses the idea in contemporary terms.

He wasted little time getting to the point of his message. And when he began, he sounded like a battle-worn cynic who had lost his capacity for joy. "The words of the Teacher, son of David, king in Jerusalem: 'Meaningless! Meaningless!' says the Teacher. 'Utterly meaningless! Everything is meaningless'" (Eccles. 1:1,2).

This certainly does not sound like what we might expect to hear from a man who is about to challenge us to live for God! His words sound more like the cynical counsel of a much later philosopher from France, named Camus, who said that life is a bad joke.

Solomon's observations about life, however, will not turn out false or depressing. As one reads through Ecclesiastes, it is the *realism* of his words that is striking. They take on a tone of brutal honesty.

What Solomon seems to be doing throughout this short book is showing us what life is like from two distinct points of view—from the one who fears the Lord and from the one who does not. But he plays the game by the secularist's rules. He shows us what life is like when we consider only the evidence that our senses give us.

"Utterly meaningless! Everything is meaningless." Why "meaningless"? The word means "vapor, breath"—something transitory and unsubstantial. You cannot grasp breath. It eludes you.

If all you can believe in is what you can see and touch and prove, and if all you can prove about life is that it is here and then it is gone, then everything is like vapor or breath.

So far Solomon has only asserted his thesis. As we continue reading, we see that he does not shrink from its implications. He looks at four area of life—work, nature, the senses, history—to see what they might teach about the meaning of life.

Work

Several years ago when I was in my twenties, a friend and I decided we needed some additional income. We began to look for a car in bad repair that could be bought cheap, fixed up, and sold for a good profit. It took little time to find a car in bad repair! We named it the Blue Ox, for obvious reasons, and began our work on it as soon as it was ours.

As we repaired one defect, we would find something else that needed work. Our investment became increasingly expensive. Finally, after several weeks' work, we were ready to sell the Blue Ox and make our fortunes.

We ran our ad in the newspaper, but to no avail.

Finally, we had to lower our price, and eventually we sold the car. When we sat down that night to pay off our bills and total the amount we had gained, each of us had a profit of $35.00! We learned a good lesson about old cars and fast dollars, but we had very little gain.

Have you seen the television commercial where a bright

young man in a three-piece suit admits to the viewers, "I am making more money now than I ever have. But I have nothing to show for it"? Ever feel that way? Solomon did. He knew all about working hard and coming up empty-handed.

> What does man gain from all his labor at which he toils
> under the sun? Generations come and generations go,
> but the earth remains forever (1:3,4).

When Solomon uses the word *gain* here, he is using it in the same way we do. It is a Hebrew word taken from the ancient business world, and it means money gained from work rendered. "When I've done my work, what's left for me?" We all understand that question. It is a fair one. Even Jesus used the same imagery when He asked, "What good is it for a man to gain the whole world, yet forfeit his soul?" (Mark 8:36).

When he uses the word *labor*, Solomon is speaking of hard work. No air-conditioned offices, company cars, or any of the other modern perks here! Since the fall of humanity, we have been called to toil (see Gen. 3:17-19). The command, "Six days you shall labor" comes before "the seventh day is a Sabbath . . . . On it you shall not do any work" (Exod. 20:9,10). We need to worship God, and we need to work. Both are important.

But what is the point of our toil? Verse 4 of Ecclesiastes 1 adds the next dark stroke: "Generations come and generations go, but the earth remains forever." The word *earth* means the dirt on which we walk. It outlasts us! We, who are made in the image of God and are the pinnacle of His creation, will be survived by the very dirt from which we are molded. This has happened for generations; it will happen to us.

So what do we accomplish when we go to the office—or wherever we go—to do whatever toil is ours? And what is our toil going to mean? What is the gain? What is the profit? When the transaction is over, when all the taxes and Social Security and hospitalization insurance and retirement benefits have been withheld, what do I take home?

> Yet when I surveyed all that my hands had done and

what I had toiled to achieve, everything was meaningless, a chasing after the wind; nothing was gained
under the sun (Eccles. 2:11).

No profit. No gain. Solomon had spent so much of his life
chasing the wind. "It was all meaningless!" he concludes. Who
ever really catches the wind? Who ever grasps everything he or
she wants? And even if we are fortunate enough to amass a fortune from our toil, over the long run our efforts are still futile.
"Naked a man comes from his mother's womb, and as he comes,
so he departs. He takes nothing from his labor that he can carry
in his hand" (5:15).

We came into this world with nothing; we will be just as rich
when we leave it. Then why are we engaged in this feverish
activity, especially when in the end it turns out like the Blue Ox?

That is life's verdict for the secularist who faces the implications of what he or she believes. We live. We work. We die. And
the beat goes on.

But wait a minute! How about us who believe, who inhabit
the kingdom of God? Solomon forces the Christian to look at
work and ask what the profit is. Is there any eternal gain that can
accrue to our toil? Surely there must be a godly motive in hauling
off to work each day.

Four Objectives for Our Work

Let me suggest four reasons why we should work. First, *we
work to bring glory to God.* "Whatever you do, do it all for the
glory of God" (1 Cor. 10:31). The quality of our work, the integrity with which we do it, and the love we show while doing it—
all can bring glory to God.

One of the most effective glorifiers of God I ever knew was a
parking-lot attendant at a well-known restaurant. An elderly
gentleman, he served his customers with more grace and enthusiasm than many of us exude who pastor churches. Another was
a lady who made wedding cakes for a living in her home kitchen.
Not only her demeanor, but the artistry and quality of her work
spoke of the order of the kingdom. So, let us glorify God in

everything we do, even in tasks that the world may call mundane.

Second, *we work to gain a livelihood.* "If a man will not work, he shall not eat" (2 Thess. 3:10). There is a joy in meeting life's basic needs through work. It is God's plan, and we are privileged to be a part of it.

Third, *we work to have wealth to share.* "He . . . must work, doing something useful with his own hands, that he may have something to share with those in need" (Eph. 4:28). Giving makes our work sacred. Why? Because when we give, we are following God's example (see John 3:16).

Tragically, one of the prime vices of the day—even among Christians—is greed. How can you combat it? The most effective way I know is by almsgiving, doling out of our abundance to those in need. Look for ways, watch for opportunities to share with the poor the excess of your wealth. One friend has a habit of keeping an eye out for young married couples whose shoe-string budgets do not allow them to have an occasional evening out. He delights in putting 25 or 30 dollars in an envelope—anonymously if possible—and sending them out to dinner.

Another friend bought a dog and gave him to a man down the street who was lonely because he lived alone. With tears of gratitude, the neighbor received his warm and wiggling gift. Be creative as you watch for ways to express your gratitude to God.

Fourth, *we work to have bridges for Christian witness.* Jesus told us to make disciples while we live (see Matt. 28:19). Most of us have many opportunities to share Christ with the people we know.

One of the great advantages a layman or woman has over those in full-time pastoral work in the area of Christian witness is *natural contact* with nonbelievers. People in normal daily working or neighborhood relationships have unforced friendships that a pastor can rarely develop.

A friend served for several years on the staff of a campus ministry. Later he accepted an administrative post at a large university. Referring to his period of employment at the university he said: "They were the richest years of evangelism I ever had. I was not 'paid' to talk about Christ. I witnessed within the system, not simply to the system."

Don't despair because your responsibilities as a wife, mother, plumber, or insurance agent limit your time for Christian service. What you may lose in *hours* available, you more than make up for in *lives* available. Take heart! You're out where the people are!

When it is done for the Lord, a Christian's work is sacred. We are not just working for money. We cannot take it with us anymore than the unbeliever can take his with him. We are not working for power or luxury. We labor to give glory to God, to sustain our lives, to be able to help others, and to build bridges for winning and discipling people to Him.

Nature

God's creation gives our lives incredible stability and continuity. A few years ago, for example, my wife and I returned to where we had spent our honeymoon. We visited the mountain streams where we had sat eighteen years earlier. We had both changed during those eighteen years, but the streams had not. Eighteen years or eighteen hundred years had not made any appreciable difference.

In like manner, when we lived in Minnesota, we enjoyed the variety of the seasons. In the fall, I looked forward to the snow covering my lawn so I would not have to mow the grass, and the cold so I would not have to repaint the house. In the winter I looked forward to spring when it would be warm and we could play golf and cook out-of-doors. In the spring I looked forward to the summer so I could be with my family, do a little fishing and traveling, or sit by a lake for quiet reflection. (This also was a good time to try to convince myself that it was wiser to paint the house in the fall than in the spring.) In the summer I looked forward to fall when things got back on schedule and the weather cooled.

Solomon understood the movements of nature, and he knew that long after we have left this earth the forces of nature will continue on in their predictable ways.

The sun rises and the sun sets, and hurries back to

where it rises. The wind blows to the south and turns
to the north; round and round it goes, ever returning
on its course. All streams flow into the sea, yet the
sea is never full" (1:5-7).

Keep in mind that Solomon is showing us how nature works,
and he is doing so from the point of view of someone who
ignores the Lord. To a person who is not honest enough to face
the fact that God made all this, nature *is* pointless. The sun rises
only to set again. The wind blows from one direction, then
another; but eventually it gets back to where it was. The
streams keep running to the same places, and those places
never get full; their sources never run dry.

So what is the point? Nature has been going its way for a
long time, and it will continue to do so long after we are gone.
That is all the secularist can ever say about the subject and
remain "objective."

The believer, on the other hand, discovers great meaning in
nature.

At sunrise or sunset I can be reminded to praise the Lord for
His blessings. "From the rising of the sun to the place where it
sets the name of the Lord is to be praised" (Ps. 113:3).

As I sit by the stream or river, I can let my soul be challenged. "As the deer pants for streams of water, so my soul
pants for you, O God" (Ps. 42:1).

I can rejoice in the drama of the storm, for my Lord is master
of even the fiercest elements of nature. "[Jesus] got up, rebuked
the wind and said to the waves, 'Quiet! Be still!' Then the wind
died down and it was completely calm . . . . They were terrified
and asked each other, 'Who is this? Even the wind and the
waves obey him!'" (Mark 4:39, 41).

When I look into space and see the vast galaxies that make
our sun and earth seem so small, I can marvel at His love for
me. "And even the very hairs of your head are all numbered"
(Matt. 10:30).

When I see the beauty of this earth, I can know that the
same One who made it is preparing another place for me. "And if
I go and prepare a place for you, I will come back and take you to

be with me that you also may be where I am" (John 14:3).

When I see the birds and flowers, I know that God has provided for them, and His provision for me is much greater. "Look at the birds of the air; they do not sow or reap or store away in barns, and yet your heavenly Father feeds them. Are you not much more valuable than they? . . . See how the lilies of the field grow. They do not labor or spin. Yet I tell you that not even Solomon in all his splendor was dressed like one of these" (Matt. 6:26,28,29).

Without a knowledge of the Lord Jesus Christ, everything in nature is so pointless. Season follows season, but nothing really changes. But to one who sees life from God's perspective, nature is full of value for time and eternity.

The Senses

Solomon continues his probing. This time he takes a look at two of our most important senses—sight and hearing.

All things are wearisome, more than one can say. The eye never has enough of seeing, or the ear its fill of hearing (1:8).

I have often thanked the Lord that I have good sight and hearing. And yet this Preacher complains that even those two senses are so filled with weariness that he cannot describe it all. Why? Because the eye is never satisfied, no matter how much it sees or how much we possess. And the ear can never hear all it wants, especially of those things that please it.

Several years ago a popular singer expressed much the same sentiment, only in a completely secular sense. She sang of young love, pleasure, marriage, children, and even life and death. At the end of each stanza, she would lament her hopeless cry that if that was all there is, then we should just get drunk and have a good time. Presumably, no matter how good something is, it is not enough. Life is just a series of disappointing experiences.

A person who does not have Christ at the center of life can

never be truly satisfied. Regardless of how much he or she sees or hears, owns or experiences, it is never enough. There will always be that craving for more. Why? *Because there is an empty spot in our lives that only God can fill.* No amount of activity or success can ever fill it in His absence.

The psalmist writes, "Delight yourself in the Lord and he will give you the desires of your heart" (Ps. 37:4). God has reserved the privilege of bringing satisfaction and meaning to our lives for Himself. We will not find it anywhere else.

History

You have heard it before. "There is nothing new under the sun." Look who said it first.

> What has been will be again, what has been done will be done again; there is nothing new under the sun. Is there anything of which one can say, "Look! This is something new"? It was here already, long ago; it was here before our time (Eccles. 1:9,10).

The French have a proverb that goes, "The more things change, the more they turn out to be the same." That is what Solomon means. He is not saying that people never invent anything new or that every object on the face of the earth is exactly as it always has been. That would be a ridiculous belief. Instead, Solomon is offering a sweeping comment on life. It is as if he is saying, "No matter how much we think we've changed things, the old ways still go on."

"What has been will be again. . . . Is there anything of which one can say, 'Look! This is something new'? It was here already, long ago." Solomon, remember, is building his case; and this time he is showing secularists the emptiness of their lives in view of the sweep of history. What has happened in the past was not unique, and neither is what is happening today.

This pointlessness extends to all history, the past and the future. Some hope to pin their hopes for meaning on the dream that they will be remembered after they die, a sort of immortality in others' minds. Listen to Solomon's warning: "There is no remembrance of men of old, and even those who are yet to come will not be remembered by those who follow" (1:11).

Humanity is not particularly interested in the past. We know some of what has gone before us, but very little of it has become a part of our memory. It has little meaning for most of us. Historians remind us of this, saying that human beings have benefited very little from the mistakes of the past. So all we learn from history is that we learn nothing from history. Similarly, it is foolish to think that future generations will be standing in line to join our fan clubs!

How pointless our lives seem in the light of history. Unless . . .

When Solomon uses the phrase *under the sun* (he uses it thirty times in Ecclesiastes), he is talking about the observable world. He is not talking about spiritual or eternal things. He is talking about the things that are important to those who live their lives believing that what they experience on earth is all there is.

Solomon is building his case with these words. Soon he will tell us what his point is, but it will not be found in the meaningless cycle of each generation reliving the story and repeating the mistakes of previous generations.

When God Is at Work

The truth is that there are new things. All of them come from the hands of a loving God.

"He put a new song in my mouth, a hymn of praise to our God. Many will see and fear and put their trust in the Lord" (Ps. 40:3).

"Behold, I will create new heavens and a new earth" (Isa. 65:17).

"I will give them an undivided heart and put a new spirit in them; I will remove from them their heart of stone and give them a heart of flesh" (Ezek. 11:19).

"Therefore, if anyone is in Christ, he is a new creation; the old has gone, the new has come!" (2 Cor. 5:17).

"He who was seated on the throne said, 'I am making everything new!' Then he said, 'Write this down, for these words are trustworthy and true'" (Rev. 21:5).

There is so much that is new when God is at work.

In the New Testament we are told that our lives do have significance. The apostle Paul talked of living all his life in the light of eternity: "I press on toward the goal to win the prize for which God has called me heavenward in Christ Jesus" (Phil. 3:14). He lived under the assumption that the important things are those which are unseen: "So we fix our eyes not on what is seen, but on what is unseen. For what is seen is temporary, but what is unseen is eternal" (2 Cor. 4:18).

Solomon has driven home his point: the one who does not live by belief in God hopes against hope. In that condition life can only be meaningless—fleeting, vaporous, "vanity." Only a belief in the one true God will give anyone a basis for hope or a meaningful life.

Just as surely, since Christ is God's giving of Himself to us, those who put Him at the center of their lives transcend the hopelessness of work, nature, the senses, and history. Jesus said, "I am the way and the truth and the life" (John 14:6).

It is still true.

Questions for Discussion

1. Review the author's four objectives for work. Then, evaluate your own work. Do the daily tasks you perform meet the four objectives? If not, what can you do to improve?
2. Romans 1:20 says that God's creation reveals His invisible qualities. How have you found this to be true?
3. What satisfaction can be found through the senses? What is the most meaningful thing you have ever seen or heard?
4. Historians claim that humanity repeats the mistakes of history, instead of learning from them. Ecclesiastes 1:9-11 seems to agree. Have you found this to be true as well? What mistakes of the past have you been inclined to make?
5. What "new things" from the hands of a loving God have you received recently? How have these new things changed your life and relationship with the Lord?

CHAPTER TWO

Where Am I to Find Happiness and Satisfaction?

Ecclesiastes 1:12–2:26

All of us have restless hearts. There is something in us that is never really satisfied, never content. We want more. We want better. We want.

A friend told me of a sales job he held several years ago. Unsure of himself, he worked harder and longer than the rest of the sales staff to prove himself. Beginning with the company's poorest sales territory, he turned it into the second best before his first year was completed. From that time on, until the day he burned out and collapsed, he never had less than a 100 percent increase in sales each year. "I would go in for my annual review each December," he said, "and my boss would look at my sales figures, grin, and say, 'I've only got one word to say. *More!*'"

Shaking his head, my friend smiled, "You know, I should have been mad. I was already doing the best job in the company. But it never bothered me, because it was the same word that haunted me every day of the year. More! I drove myself over the edge. I can't blame anyone else. I was just never satisfied with what I did, even when it was the best."

King Solomon had more. Because he was a king, he could try everything in life his heart desired. And after having searched the same places we search—intellectual pursuits, pleasure, social and material achievement—he concluded that there was no real satisfaction to be found in any of them.

So he decided to conduct an experiment.

We understand experiments. From our youth we are taught how to test ideas, see if they work, evaluate them, and draw our conclusions. Watch Solomon as he tests life to see if there is any satisfaction to be found in the places where we all look.

"I, the Teacher, was king over Israel in Jerusalem. I devoted myself to study and to explore by wisdom all that is done under heaven. What a heavy burden God has laid on men! I have seen all the things that are done under the sun; all of them are meaningless, a chasing after the wind. What is twisted cannot be straightened; what is lacking cannot be counted" (Eccles. 1:12-15).

Solomon begins his experiment by revealing his conclusion. He summarizes it and goes beyond just what may be observed in nature. He knows that all of us are restless and unsatisfied; that much can be observed. But he attributes this dissatisfaction to God: "What a heavy burden God has laid on men!" (1:13). Interestingly enough, much later the apostle Paul made much the same point: "For the creation was subjected to frustration, not by its own choice, but by the will of the one who subjected it" (Rom. 8:20).

The wisdom of which Solomon talks is human, secular wisdom. The "heavy burden" is every human activity that lacks God at the center; it is an inevitable result of living without God as the focus of one's life. It was true then. It is true now. Everything we can observe in this world is pointless in itself. It goes nowhere; it is like "chasing after the wind." Down inside we know there is more, but we cannot grasp it. Every time we think we have almost found it, it evades us.

That is what life is like.

Furthermore, we cannot change it. "What is twisted cannot be straightened; what is lacking cannot be counted" (Eccles. 1:15). *Today's English Version* says it well, "You can't straighten out what is crooked; you can't count things that aren't there." There are many things we cannot change. Life has many flaws; it always will.

Years ago, at the end of a long day of driving, I stopped for a pizza with my family. As we sat in the restaurant unwinding and enjoying the relaxed atmosphere, a young couple and their two small sons came in and sat next to us. I took one look at the situation and knew the peace and quiet was over. My mind flashed back to when our own children were young and we were someone else's disturbance. Now it was our turn to be on the receiving end. There will always be crooked things that cannot be made straight!

It was not long after this experience that I had a speaking engagement in another city. As I boarded the airplane to return home, I noticed that the businessman across the aisle in the row behind me had his attaché case open and had taken out his clipboard to do some paperwork. He appeared pleased with life, until a young woman with one baby in her arms and another in an infant seat, along with a two-year-old toddler, crowded into the two seats next to him. It seemed as if all three children cried or yelled throughout the entire flight. At one point I turned to see how he was doing. I will never forget the look on his face. It was as if he had received a painful, fatal injection and was waiting for it to take effect.

There will always be problems and annoyances in our lives that simply cannot be corrected. Tired, afraid, upset babies will always be with us, God bless them! So will sickness, hatred, injustice, and untimely death.

The bad news is that it will always be that way. Even the best things in life have their defects. But the good news is that they do not have to affect your inner joy. External circumstances do not make or break us; how we handle them is far more important.

The Experiment

Solomon begins to examine the best things the observable world has to offer us. They are the things that we still seek today; and if we will look over his shoulder as he conducts his experiment, we will gain the benefit of his experience.

First, Solomon examines *wisdom*. Keep in mind, he is looking at the observable world, the world apart from God, the world

"under the sun." We need to distinguish the wisdom he is evalu-
ating—human knowledge—from true wisdom, which comes
from God (see Prov. 9:10) and matures us to see things as God
does (1 Cor. 2:6-16).

"I thought to myself, 'Look, I have grown and increased in
wisdom more than anyone who has ruled over Jerusalem before
me; I have experienced much of wisdom and knowledge.' Then I
applied myself to the understanding of wisdom, and also of madness and folly, but I learned that this, too, is a chasing after the
wind. For with much wisdom comes much sorrow; the more
knowledge, the more grief" (Eccles. 1:16-18).

What did he discover? After probing wisdom "to know wisdom and to know madness and folly"—that is, so he could be
wise rather than foolish—he declared "this, too, is a chasing
after the wind." Why? The more he learned, the more reason he
had for grief and sorrow. The clearer he could think, the more
clearly he could see how easily life can go wrong and that nothing
on earth is permanent.

The more we learn, the more we realize how little we know.
As we discover new information, we see whole areas where we
know nothing and in which we can never hope to learn anything.
We realize that we live in a world where our knowledge is limited
and our ability to control the future is an illusion.

The more we learn, the clearer we see how precarious life
really is. All of us die (see 2:15); eventually time and chance get
to us (see 9:11,12); we never know whether once we are gone
our efforts will prosper or fail (see 2:19). There are no guarantees; and the more clearly we look at life, the more vividly we
see that.

The more we know, the more we see how we make mistake
after mistake. Our blunders are embarrassing; they also bring us
much grief.

More knowledge does not necessarily lead to more enlightened living; frequently it leads to greater evil. We live in the day
of the knowledge explosion, and yet humanity is closer than ever
to destroying itself with war, violence, and brutality. As one
skeptic has said, "Modern technology has only served to make
us more efficient in our cruelty."

We Christians need to be careful here. Further education is fine; it may be smack in the center of God's will for you. But don't ever use your pursuit of knowledge to provide the satisfaction and peace that can be found only in Christ and His kingdom. The enemy of our souls can easily take an M.A. or Ph.D. after our names and make it an idol.

So what do we do? I believe in getting a good education. We should encourage our children in school. We should continue learning as adults. But scholarly wisdom that has no room for God at its center is of no ultimate value. We must seek the wisdom that comes from God.

Second, Solomon examines *pleasure*. Why not? We can relate to pleasure! We live in a time when there are more pleasures available—good and bad—than we could ever experience. Our society is saturated with the pursuit of pleasure.

"I thought in my heart, 'Come now, I will test you with pleasure to find out what is good.' But that also proved to be meaningless. 'Laughter,' I said, 'is foolish. And what does pleasure accomplish?' I tried cheering myself with wine, and embracing folly—my mind still guiding me with wisdom. I wanted to see what was worthwhile for men to do under heaven during the few days of their lives" (2:1-3).

Who could test pleasure more thoroughly than a king? Solomon had more wealth and power than anyone, so why not? If wisdom will not give us what we expect from it, let's escape into hedonism. Solomon's conclusion? "That also proved to be meaningless" (2:1).

In another place Solomon wrote, "A cheerful heart is good medicine" (Prov. 17:22). So he is not making light of the value of entertainment or laughter, only of expecting more from it than it can provide. Laughter can be therapeutic. We need it. But when it is what we live for, when it is a goal of our lives rather than a result, it eludes us.

So why not get drunk? "I tried cheering myself with wine" (Eccles. 2:3). Surely he knew better. He himself had painted a vivid picture of the alcohol-saturated life.

Who has woe: Who has sorrow? Who has strife? Who

has complaints? Who has needless bruises? Who has bloodshot eyes? Those who linger over wine, who go to sample bowls of mixed wine. Do not gaze at wine when it is red, when it sparkles in the cup, when it goes down smoothly! In the end it bites like a snake and poisons like a viper. Your eyes will see strange sights and your mind imagine confusing things. You will be like one sleeping on the high seas, lying on top of the rigging. "They hit me," you will say, "but I'm not hurt! They beat me, but I don't feel it!" (Prov. 23:29-35).

With the large numbers of automobile accidents, divorce, and child abuse cases related to drinking, it is obvious that people continue to seek pleasure through drunkenness. And it is no less vain and empty today than it was in Solomon's time.

Note that Solomon does not say it is wrong to enjoy ourselves. We need pleasure, just as we need knowledge. But the apostle Paul's advice holds true: "So whether you eat or drink or whatever you do, do it all for the glory of God" (1 Cor. 10:31). We are to live for God's glory. When we do so, all of life will be sacred, including our pleasure. But pleasure will not bring us the satisfaction we desire.

Third, Solomon examines *achievement*. He has covered the bases now. If you find someone who is not immersed in education or pleasure, chances are he or she is striving for success. Millions look for their satisfaction here, especially if they have tried the others and found them wanting. Could so many people be wrong? Listen to Solomon's words:

"I undertook great projects: I built houses for myself and planted vineyards. I made gardens and parks and planted all kinds of fruit trees in them. I made reservoirs to water groves of flourishing trees. I bought male and female slaves and had other slaves who were born in my house. I also owned more herds and flocks than anyone in Jerusalem before me. I amassed silver and gold for myself, and the treasure of kings and provinces. I acquired men and women singers, and a harem as well—the delights of the heart of man. I became greater by far than anyone in Jerusalem before me. In all this my wisdom stayed with me. I denied myself nothing my eyes desired; I refused my heart no pleasure. My heart took delight in all my work, and this was the reward for all my labor. Yet when I surveyed all that my hands had done and what I had toiled to achieve, everything was meaningless, a chasing after the wind; nothing was gained under the sun" (Eccles. 2:4-11).

Solomon tried to create his own Garden of Eden. He built houses and vineyards and parks and orchards. He made pools and bought slaves and herds and flocks. He accumulated silver and gold, musicians and concubines. He indulged every whim and satisfied every appetite imaginable. Very few persons could match his ability to give the acid test to achievement. If anyone could find satisfaction in his accomplishments, certainly King Solomon would have done so. Even our modern millionaires, with all their wealth, could not outdo him.

He even enjoyed his job! But what was Solomon's verdict?

> Yet when I surveyed all that my hands had done and
> what I had toiled to achieve, everything was meaning-
> less, a chasing after the wind; nothing was gained
> under the sun (2:11).

"It's not here either! I still haven't found anything worthwhile. It's all vanity, empty. Achievement is empty. Possessions are like grasping at the wind. Nothing can be gained from them."

How good of God to share this experiment with us! We can learn from it and not make the same mistakes.

But we can learn from our pasts, too. Remember that object you just *had* to have. You positively knew it would bring satisfaction. Did it? Of course not.

Solomon's Evaluation of Human Desire

So far Solomon has been very harsh on the things that people desire the most—knowledge, pleasure, achievement. He now doubles back over his experiment to evaluate and explain just why it turned out as it did. He begins with wisdom and pleasure, or folly.

> Then I turned my thoughts to consider wisdom, and
> also madness and folly. What more can the king's suc-
> cessor do than what has already been done? I saw that
> wisdom is better than folly, just as light is better than
> darkness. The wise man has eyes in his head, while
> the fool walks in the darkness; but I came to realize
> that the same fate overtakes them both. Then I
> thought in my heart, "The fate of the fool will over-
> take me also. What then do I gain by being wise?" I
> said in my heart, "This too is meaningless." For the
> wise man, like the fool, will not be long remembered;
> in days to come both will be forgotten. Like the fool,
> the wise man too must die! So I hated life, because
> the work that is done under the sun was grievous to
> me. All of it is meaningless, a chasing after the wind
> (Eccles. 2:12-17).

Solomon had been testing wisdom and folly in his experiment. He recognized that we might be tempted to doubt the truth of his experiment; so he reminds us, "What more can the king's successor do than what has already been done?" It is as if he is saying, "Come on, now. I'm a hard act to follow. What are you going to try that I haven't done? In fact, you can only do *some* of what I've done."

Even wisdom without God is better than foolishness without Him. It is as much better as light is to darkness (see 2:13). A wise person has his eyes "in his head," but a fool walks around as though his eyes are shut (see 2:14).

And yet, there is a problem. It is a simple one: we are human beings, and we will die. If "the same fate overtakes them both ... what then do I gain by being wise?" (2:14,15). If the wise person and the fool suffer the same fate, why seek wisdom? To add insult to injury, Solomon reminds us that both the fool and the wise person "will be forgotten" in the future. No one will even remember them.

What is more mortifying about our mortality than this! It mocks everything important to us.

There is a solution. In chapter 3, verse 11, Solomon gives his answer. What we see here is not the whole picture. If we eliminate God from our lives, the gloomy view is the right one. But when we live for God, life takes on new meaning.

There is a godly wisdom that makes all the difference in the world. The book of Daniel speaks of it: "Those who are wise will shine like the brightness of the heavens, and those who lead many to righteousness, like the stars for ever and ever" (Dan. 12:3). And in Revelation 14:13 we are told, concerning those who died in the Lord, "'Blessed are the dead who die in the Lord from now on. Yes,' says the Spirit, 'they will rest from their labor, for their deeds will follow them.'"

The fact that Solomon was bitter about this cruel hoax—"So I hated life" (Eccles. 2:17)—also says something about the solution to the dilemma it poses. It almost reaches forward to the marvelous words of chapter 3, "He has also set eternity in the hearts of men" (v. 11), to declare Solomon's faith and explain where satisfaction can be found.

Solomon is not ready to quit his experiment. He wants to keep at it. So he returns to humanity's achievements. But even there, only bitterness is to be found. "I hated all the things I had toiled for under the sun, because I must leave them to the one who comes after me. And who knows whether he will be a wise man or a fool? Yet he will have control over all the work into which I have poured my effort and skill under the sun. This too is meaningless. So my heart began to despair over all my toilsome labor under the sun. For a man may do his work with wisdom, knowledge and skill, and then he must leave all he owns to someone who has not worked for it. This too is meaningless and a great misfortune. What does a man get for all the toil and anxious striving with which he labors under the sun? All his days his work is pain and grief; even at night his mind does not rest. This too is meaningless" (2:18-23).

Remember now, he was the king. It is not as if he were under-employed. Being king is not a bad job! But he is angry— *mad*! "It really angers me," he is saying. "I'm going to work hard all my life. I'm going to amass a fortune, and someone else will get it. I don't like that at all." And furthermore, "He might be a fool and waste it." In fact, that is exactly what Solomon's son Rehoboam did. He played the fool and took poor advice, and his kingdom was split (see 1 Kings 12).

There is an interesting lesson to be found here. Solomon talks about the man whose consuming passion is his work; he has so much on his mind that he cannot sleep at night (see Eccles. 2:23). The psalmist wrote, "In vain you rise early and stay up late, toiling for food to eat—for he grants sleep to those he loves" (Ps. 127:2). God wants us to work, but He wants us to order our priorities and not make an idol of our work.

Jesus had the best plan when He said, "Come to me, all you who are weary and burdened, and I will give you rest" (Matt. 11:28). He did not mean that we would no longer need to work and could lie around all day. He will give us rest *in* our work. "Take my yoke upon you . . . and you will find rest for your souls. For my yoke is easy and my burden is light" (Matt. 11:29,30). It is still a yoke; but it is the yoke of Jesus, and it fits. It does not chafe. It is good, for there is rest for our souls in the midst of our labor.

I have often thought of how Jesus lived His life. As far as I can tell, He was never in a hurry and He never wasted time. When I am in a hurry, I am going faster than He is. When I am wasting time—and I am not talking about relaxation or entertainment—I am a poor steward. Jesus never gives us more to do than He gives us time to do it. John Wesley said, "Though I am always in haste, I am never in a hurry, because I never undertake more work than I can go through with calmness of spirit."

Satisfaction

What is Solomon's conclusion to the matter? He repeats this message in Ecclesiastes 9:7-10 and in 11:7-10, but his basic point is that satisfaction comes in receiving God's gifts and using them for the purpose He intends. "A man can do nothing better than to eat and drink and find satisfaction in his work. This too, I see, is from the hand of God, for without him, who can eat or find enjoyment? To the man who pleases him, God gives wisdom, knowledge and happiness, but to the sinner he gives the task of gathering and storing up wealth to hand it over to the one who pleases God. This too is meaningless, a chasing after the wind" (2:24-26).

Verse 24 can be translated from Hebrew to English as, "There is nothing inherent in men and women that allows them to enjoy eating and drinking and finding enjoyment in their toil." Let me say it another way: "Man has nothing within himself that allows him to enjoy life." We cannot enjoy life apart from God.

That is the sum of the matter.

The experiment is a failure, as far as secular man is concerned. What began as a grand program to discover all those wonderful areas of life where we can be the masters of our fates and the captains of our souls has been reduced to the simple fact that we do not have the ability to find satisfaction in anything!

Satisfaction is a gift from God, just like salvation. When we can take our knowledge, our pleasure, and our work as gifts from God, then our search has found its goal. And all the good things God has in store for us are ours.

Death will take away none of that satisfaction.

There is a crowning irony in the last verse of this chapter. Notice the contrast between what God gives—wisdom, knowledge, and joy—and what humanity strives so hard to amass but cannot keep. Even that, we are told, will go to the righteous. But the righteous have their treasure in heaven (see Matt. 6:21). Their hearts will be there, too.

Questions for Discussion

1. Have you, like the salesman described by the author, been pursuing more, instead of pursuing what is best? What actions must you take to apply Solomon's wisdom about this matter to your life?
2. How has the pursuit of knowledge or wisdom affected your

life? Have you seen improvement or disintegration in your commitment to the Lord and His wisdom?

3. To what extent does the pursuit of pleasure characterize life in our society?

4. Has seeking achievement brought you satisfaction? Why? Why not?

5. Do you agree with Solomon's conclusion that satisfaction comes in receiving God's gifts and using them for the purpose He intends? Why? Why not?

CHAPTER THREE

How Can I Fit Into God's Plans?

Ecclesiastes 3:1-15

In his book, *Born Again*, Charles Colson told of his conversion to Christ following the reelection of President Nixon and the accompanying scandals that shocked the world.

The book opened with a revealing election-night scene that preceded Colson's troubles with the Watergate prosecutors. Standing in the elegant Washington, D.C., hotel, he realized that they had managed an unprecedented landslide victory. At the same time, he was puzzled over the uneasiness that was gnawing at him even in his moment of triumph.

Later that night, after several hours alone with the president of the United States, he realized that something was seriously wrong. A deadness was eating away at him; even the most exhilarating of human achievements could not hide it.

There is something in each of us that says there has to be more to life than what we see and experience. So much of what we do seems meaningless over the long run. We mow the grass; it grows and we have to mow it again. We clean the house; it gets dirty and we have to clean it again. We go to work, pick up a pay check, and spend it; we go back to work so we can pick up another pay check and spend it. We cook all day, or so it seems, to eat our meals; the next day we do it all over again.

If you are like me, every once in a while you look at all this activity and say, "What is the point of it all? Why am I doing this?" Surely, life has to be more than mowing grass, cleaning house, working, cooking eating. We want to give our lives to more than this; we want them to be meaningful.

Solomon understood that feeling. He undoubtedly experienced it himself. And he knew that the secular-minded person feels it, too. So, as a part of his ongoing apologetic for the spiritual life, he painted another vivid word picture. In this picture he declares that God's plan encompasses everything, even mowing lawns and cleaning house and changing diapers and earning a living. All of it.

God's All-Encompassing Plan

There is a time for everything,
and a season for every activity under heaven (3:1).

At first glance it is reassuring to know that "there is a right time for everything," as *The Living Bible* reads. To illustrate his statement, Solomon then proceeds to list fourteen pairs of opposites that are a part of God's plan that we must acknowledge.

a time to be born and a time to die, a time to plant and
a time to uproot, a time to kill and a time to heal, a
time to tear down and a time to build, a time to weep
and a time to laugh, a time to mourn and a time to
dance, a time to scatter stones and a time to gather
them, a time to embrace and a time to refrain, a time
to search and a time to give up, a time to keep and a
time to throw away, a time to tear and a time to mend,
a time to be silent and a time to speak, a time to love
and a time to hate, a time for war and a time for peace
(3:2-8).

This list must have driven Solomon's secular adversary wild! While there is something very comforting about the rhythmic regularity he reports, this regularity has some disturbing implications. First, if everything is part of God's plan and has its time, then I must not be as free as I thought. Someone or something bigger than I must be calling the shots or making the rules. After all, I have very little choice about the circumstances that cause me to weep or to laugh.

Second, and equally devastating, this list implies that nothing I do has permanence. "If I'm only going to die, why be born? And if what I build up will only break down, why bother doing anything?" While the believer (who knows who is in charge) finds great comfort in this regularity, it is a devastating problem for the person who leaves God out of the picture.

Solomon knew this, and his adversary knew it. So do the purveyors of our popular culture who lament the hopelessness they experience without God while they continue their dance of death, stubbornly refusing to acknowledge Him in any meaningful way.

For a moment let us look at the end of the book where Solomon gives us the key to his logic. How can he look at this endless cycle and see freedom and meaning where the secular man can only see slavery and meaninglessness? The basis for Solomon's security lies in these words:

> Now all has been heard; here is the conclusion of the
> matter: Fear God and keep his commandments, for
> this is the whole duty of man. For God will bring every
> deed into judgment, including every hidden thing,
> whether it is good or evil (12:13,14).

That is the key: God is in charge. The one who fears God, or honors Him, and keeps His commandments can be secure in the gracious love of the One who created him. That is where the difference lies.

It is interesting to observe the contrasts in these verses. God's plan includes our birth and our death (see 3:2), both of which are beyond our control, as well as the growing and harvesting of crops. It includes killing—perhaps a reference to war or executing those who have taken the life of one made in God's image (see Gen. 9:6)—and healing, as well as times when families and nations are divided and times when they are strengthened (see Eccles. 3:3. Jer. 18:7-10 also includes an interesting example of this).

God's plan includes times for sorrow and for joy, times for mourning and for celebration (see Eccles. 3:4). This is an interesting example of Hebrew poetry, for the two lines of this verse are precisely parallel. The poetry is in the idea instead of in the sound of the words, as in a rhyme.

The first half of verse 5 has puzzled interpreters. Many have assumed that it is meant literally; there is a time to throw stones (as in rocks) and a time to pick them up for building walls and buildings. Others suggest that the "time to scatter stones" refers to incidents like those that appear in 2 Kings 3:19,25, where God commanded the Israelites to tear down the cities of the Moabites and make their fields unuseable by littering them with the stones.

Jewish rabbis, however, have long taught a more likely interpretation, for they see the word "stones" as a euphemism for male testes and therefore find the first half of the verse saying that there is a time to have intercourse ("scatter stones")—for instance, when one's wife is "clean" according to the Law—and there is a time to refrain from intercourse ("gather them")—for instance, when one's wife is menstrually "unclean." (See. Lev. 12:2; 15:24; 18:19; 20:18 for specific mention of this in the Law.)

If this interpretation is correct, then the second half of the verse, which refers to embracing and refraining from embracing, would be parallel with the first half. This would make verse 5 of Ecclesiastes 3 consistent with verses 2-8, in which the second part of each verse deals with the same subject as the first.

I believe this is what Solomon was saying: "There are appropriate and inappropriate times for sexual love." There are times when it is inappropriate for married couples to engage in sexual relations, whether for medical, emotional, or other reasons. Solomon was not, as such, addressing the issue of moral purity; he was speaking of ritual purity. At the same time, while Christians today are no longer bound to Old Testament laws of ritual purity, we would do well to remember that the laws of moral purity are clearly reaffirmed by the writers of the New Testament and by

Jesus Himself. Indeed, Jesus made a point of calling His followers to a very high view of sex; sex is reserved exclusively for one's mate, and our thoughts are to be as pure as our actions are to be upright (see Matt. 5:27-32).

God's plan includes gain and loss (see Eccles. 3:6), an interesting comment in view of Solomon's statement in 1:3 that there is no profit, no gain. Similarly, there is a time to guard what we have and a time to give away our possessions. God's plan includes mourning and ceasing one's mourning (see v. 7); the reference to tearing one's clothes probably refers to the custom of tearing one's garments as an expression of grief and mending them when the time of mourning was complete (see 2 Samuel 13:31 for an example of this custom).

There are times when it is best to speak, and other times when it is prudent to remain silent, or when it is a waste of one's efforts to speak (see Eccles. 3:7).

Even the calamities of life are in God's plan. The love and hate mentioned in verse 8 do not refer to personal relationships so much as to affairs among the nations. There is also "a time for war" when God takes up the sword to destroy the wicked nations of the earth, and a time in His plan when peace is to rule.

Several years ago a popular song, "Turn, Turn, Turn," used these verses for its lyrics. As the secular world usually does, it turned the meaning of this passage on its head. Wedding its beautiful and haunting melody to these words, it lamented, "I hope we're not too late" (to stop the war).

I use this illustration to show how devastating to secular people is the idea that in God's plan there is a time for *everything.* I dislike war as much as anyone; I hate it. I believe God does, too, even when He has to use it to bring judgment among the nations. But even our greatest plans fail (see v. 6). People die and wars erupt, and only the person who trusts in the goodness of God can look it all in the face and know that somehow it is contained in the providence of God. This is not to say that the Lord plans our troubles, but He permits them. He makes everything work together with all life's experiences for good.

People with a temporal value system have trouble understanding God's providence. It is as difficult for the secular mind today as it was in Solomon's time; but, nevertheless, it is still true. God can be trusted to accomplish His own purposes!

God Makes Even the Unlovely Beautiful

At best, we see only a small part of what is happening in God's world. God's plan is not chaos; it is purposeful change. It has a beginning and an end. Everything fits together. "What does the worker gain from his toil? I have seen the burden God has laid on men. He has made everything beautiful in its time. He has also set eternity in the hearts of men; yet they cannot fathom what God has done from beginning to end" (3:9-11).

Again we return to the theme of Ecclesiastes 1:3: "What does man gain from all his labor at which he toils under the sun?" After all the seasons are over, what is my profit? What have I gained? And, as Solomon has done repeatedly, he forces the secularist to confront all those opposites that neutralize each other. "If I'm here and then die, it would make just as much sense if I hadn't been born at all, wouldn't it?" (This may, in fact, be the basis on which the secular mind justifies abortion: What difference does it make?) "If there is a time for sewing and a time for tearing, why bother sewing? What profit, what point is there in doing anything?"

Having exposed the moral bankruptcy of a secular viewpoint, Solomon presses home the point he wishes to make. "I've seen these opposites. I know they are real. But God has ordained them, and 'He has made everything beautiful in its time.'"

The word *beautiful* has a wider meaning than aesthetic beauty; it also means "appropriate." God has made everything appropriate for its time; it all fits. So when each part of our lives "fits" God's plan, it is beautiful, appropriate. Romans 8:28 says the same thing: "And we know that in all things God works for the good of those who love him, who have been called according to his purpose."

Neither Solomon nor the apostle Paul say that we will like everything in life. We might even become the victims of murder, war, or business failure. That is in God's hands. But—happy days or sad, good circumstances or evil—when all our life is within God's plan, it is appropriate and beautiful for the person who fears God and keeps His commandments (see Eccles. 12:13).

Let me illustrate this. If you go to a large state or county fair, you will notice that some of the heavy-equipment companies bring a very unusual object along with their displays. They bring a model of a transmission cut away so you can see the gears at work. Some gears go in one direction, and others go another; but they all work together to make the axle go in the direction the person operating the vehicle chooses.

When looking at the gears in a machine, people often wonder, "How can one gear go this way, one another, and others go theirs, and yet the axle turns the wheel the right direction?" Someone designed it to work that way.

Life works like that engine. Some things go our way, and some things appear to go against us. Actually, who are we to know which is which? We experience all sorts of events, and for the life of us we cannot tell how it is working together for good. But it is. It is beautiful. It is appropriate.

God made it that way.

Being born and dying. Weeping and laughing. Sewing and tearing. Planting and reaping. Killing and healing. War and peace. God is big enough to handle all of it.

God's Plan Requires Us to Return to Him

Several years ago a man sailed from the United States to England in a one-person rowboat. In the celebration that followed his arrival, a reporter asked his wife if she had been afraid he would fail. "Oh, no," she replied. "I know the one who made the boat."

It is important to know the One who made the plan. It is important to know what He is like. "He has also set eternity in the hearts of men; yet they cannot fathom what God has done from beginning to end" (3:11).

Solomon says God has put eternity in our hearts. What is that "eternity"? It is that part of you that says, "I am made for more than all this. Yes. I sow and reap and clean and cook and eat. But the clothes are going to wear out, and I will have to harvest the grain again next year, and the house will get dirty, and I will have to prepare my meals again tomorrow. But I do not live for that!"

God has put within us the knowledge that this world is not enough. He created us to have intellectual curiosity, but he did not give us the capacity to know everything about life. We cannot know how all of life fits together. No one can fathom what God has done from beginning to end (see 3:11). How wonderful! Frequently someone says to me, "I don't know how that fits into God's plan for my life." And I say, "I don't either, but God does." That should be enough for all of us. If we knew all that God knows, what kind of God would we have?

We are very much like the desperately nearsighted person who has to inch himself along a great mural. He sees enough to know it is a great work of art, but he cannot step back to see how it fits together. He sees some of this and some of that, but he cannot see all of it. We are like that. We inch along through life like a nearsighted art connoisseur. We see some bright colors and say, "Oh, how lovely. Isn't God good?" Then we see some dark, ominous clouds and we say, "How could that be part of a beautiful work of art?" Those who live in relationship with God know the one who painted the mural. We realize that the great work of art that God is making in our lives requires the dark and ominous colors along with the bright ones.

We are to rejoice and enjoy life; it is God's gift to us. The times of weeping and the times of rejoicing both come from God. We can trust the Painter. We "know the One who made the boat."

It's All Forever

The truth expressed in verses 12-15 contain very different meanings for the believer and the unbeliever. "I know that there is nothing better for men than to be happy and do good while they live. That every man may eat and drink, and find satisfaction in all his toil—this is the gift of God. I know that everything God does will endure forever; nothing can be added to it and nothing taken from it. God does it, so men will revere him. Whatever is has already been, and what will be has been before; and God will call the past to account."

For the unbeliever, these words signify utter hopelessness. Since everything is God's gift (see v. 13) and we cannot add to or subtract from God's work (see v. 14), the unbeliever is trapped in a system that cannot bend or break.

To the modern secular mind, verses 14 and 15 are a cry of despair. There is no hope, no exit (to borrow a phrase from the French existentialist philosopher, Jean-Paul Sartre). Existence is a closed system for the unbeliever; he cannot escape it or make it bend or break. Therefore, this message becomes a severe burden. "Consider therefore the kindness and sternness of God: sternness to those who fell, but kindness to you, provided that you continue in his kindness" (Rom. 11:22).

But it is a far different story for the one who knows God. If God is love (see 1 John 4:8), then nothing is in vain (in contrast to human efforts; Eccles. 1:3); for His love lasts forever. The times of weeping and of laughter both come from Him. His plans need no mid-course corrections (see Eccles. 3:14).

Earlier, in describing the world as secular men and women experience it, Solomon said, "Life is so vain. It does not last; it is transitory." But now, speaking of the truth and not describing the predicament of the one who ignores God, he says, "As a matter of fact, life is not temporary. What God does lasts forever." It is only because of our limited vision that the events of life seem so disjointed.

Why is life like that? "God does it, so men will revere him" (3:14). In several other verses in Ecclesiastes, Solomon says we are to fear God (see 5:7; 7:18; 8:12,13 [three times]; 12:13). Why is it so important for us to fear the Lord?

First, remember the commandment, "You shall have no other gods before me" (Exod. 20:3). God alone is God. He alone knows everything. If we knew what He knows, then we would be as God (see Isa. 14:14). Indeed, we would be God.

But even more important, the fear of God represents a relationship of love. In thanking God for His provision of forgiveness, the psalmist says, "But with you there is forgiveness;

therefore you are feared" (Ps. 130:4). The fear of God is a response of love for His goodness in creating us and in forgiving us of our sin. To fear God is to love Him, to commit ourselves to Him without reservation, and to say, "Lord, you alone are Lord. And I love you."

We do not always see that everything is beautiful, or appropriate. But we can believe it because of what we know about God. Knowing His character, and knowing Him personally, gives us the basis for the faith that "He has made everything beautiful in its time."

Questions for Discussion

1. When have you experienced the ebb and flow of life, as Solomon describes it in Ecclesiastes 3:1-8? Do you find this constant, pendulum-like description of life comforting or disconcerting? Why?
2. Interpreters have been puzzled by Ecclesiastes 3:5 for many years. How do you feel this verse is best explained?
3. Do you agree with Solomon that God's plan includes a time for *everything*—even war, death, mourning, and hate? Why? Why not?
4. How have you seen Ecclesiastes 3:11 proven true? How has God made "everything beautiful in its time" in your life? How does this relate to God's omniscience and to Psalm 84:11?

CHAPTER FOUR

Finding Meaning in the Midst of the Struggle

Ecclesiastes 3:16–4:16 5:8,9; 7:7

There is much in this world that brings us joy. But there is also another side to the world—the dark side. Mourning and weeping are as real as singing and laughing. Anger and war are as real as love and peace. Throughout the tapestry of life there runs a dark, harsh thread that cannot be ignored. Even on our best days, the harsh realities of life affect us.

Earlier in chapter 3 Solomon reminded us that we cannot understand everything about life. "He has made everything beautiful in its time. He has also set eternity in the hearts of men; yet they cannot fathom what God has done from beginning to end" (3:11).

Life is beautiful, we are told. It is appropriate; it fits. On the other hand, none of us can see the beginning or the end to see how it fits. We know it does, by faith; but we do not know how. We are, as it were, mentally nearsighted.

We need to see these realities as God sees them. We need to see how God makes use of them so that by faith they are beautiful to us. This way of seeing is not natural for us. We are hurt by the dark side of life, as we see the unbelievable tragedies around us. Yet, by faith we trust that God has a plan.

Injustice

We regularly read of injustices in magazines and newspapers; radio and television report the latest injustices with alarming frequency. Realist that he was, Solomon saw injustice, too.

> And I saw something else under the sun: In the place
> of judgment—wickedness was there, in the place of
> justice—wickedness was there. I thought in my heart,
> "God will bring to judgment both the righteous and the
> wicked, for there will be a time for every activity, a
> time for every deed" (Eccles. 3:16,17).

These words remind us of verses 2-8, where everything is subject to reversal. Here, however, injustice of all things becomes an exception! Ironically, injustice is one reality we wish *would* be reversed. "At least here," we might say, "we can find some gain!" (See 1:3.)

God provided for human courts and tribunals to execute justice. They are part of His plan for bringing justice to a sinful world; their corruption illustrates how profoundly we need them. Our frustration lies in the fact that our days, as well as our sight, are limited; we cannot "fathom what God has done from beginning to end" (3:11). We cannot see the consequences of injustice in the immediate future.

Secularists have been getting by with injustice for thousands of years; they believe that God's justice will never prevail, if they even bother to consider the subject. But God says, "Listen, a day is coming when humanity's day will end and my day will begin."

> The wicked plot against the righteous and gnash their
> teeth at them; but the Lord laughs at the wicked, for
> he knows their day is coming (Ps. 37:12,13).

Believers know better than to despair. We know that ultimately God will judge every person's work. "For he has set a day when he will judge the world with justice by the man he has appointed" (Acts 17:31). The day has already been determined; God has declared this by raising Jesus from the dead.

Death

Death is the ultimate harsh reality. It represents finality for the person whose sole orientation is to this life; it suggests pain and sorrow even for the believer. In picking up this subject, Solomon declares that even death is "beautiful in its time." It is part of God's provision.

"I also thought, 'As for men, God tests them so that they may see that they are like the animals. Man's fate is like that of the animals; the same fate awaits them both: As one dies, so dies the other. All have the same breath; man has no advantage over the animal. Everything is meaningless. All go to the same place; all come from dust, and to dust all return'" (Eccles. 3:18-20).

Death forces us to remember that we are creatures, not the Creator. If we are like the beasts in our greed and in our mortality, then it would be wise for us to know it (see 3:18). Left to our own devices, we are likely to ignore our sinful nature. Therefore, God is merciful to remind us who we are.

Solomon is not dealing here with our eternal state (heaven or hell) once we die. And his point is not so much that we die as it is that prideful humanity dies. "God tests them so that they may see that they are like the animals" (3:18). So why should we be proud?

If we are going to limit our belief about our nature to what we can observe—and that is what Solomon is asking his secular-minded friend to do—then we are, in fact, forced to conclude that we are no better than the beasts. They die; we die. Their bodies decay; our bodies decay. They become one thing—dust (see Gen. 3:19). So do we.

Period.

For all we can see, that is the end of the matter. Or is it?

"'Who knows if the spirit of man rises upward and if the spirit of the animals goes down into the earth?' So I saw that there is nothing better for a man than to enjoy his work, because that is his lot. For who can bring him to see what will happen after him?" (Eccles. 3:21,22).

In verse 21, Solomon is clearly challenging the reader to look at what he or she sees every day, and nothing else, and tell him if he or she can observe anything different in the death of a human being and the death of an animal. Solomon knows there is a difference. He has just reminded us that we are going to die, just like the beasts. He knows that for the beast it is the end of everything, but not so for people. We cannot prove it from anything we can see, though. So, "Who knows . . . ?" That is exactly the point.

Solomon knows, and so do we. He knows that the spirits of human beings do not cease to exist at death. Yes, the body does deteriorate, just as the body of an animal decomposes; but the spirit goes to God, either for punishment or reward. Some will enjoy God's "Come and share your master's happiness!" (Matt. 25:21). Others will hear, "I never knew you. Away from me, you evildoers!" (Matt. 7:23). "Dust to dust" is not the complete story.

Death should be a comfort to the Christian. None of us desires to die, unless we are in a mental condition that has obliterated our ability to think rationally. Every Christian should be able to look at the inevitability of death and say, "I love life, but death is going to be even better than life!" That is what the apostle Paul said: "I am torn between the two: I desire to depart and be with Christ, which is better by far" (Phil. 1:23) and "I pray also that the eyes of your heart may be enlightened in order that you may know the hope to which he has called you, the riches of his glorious inheritance in the saints" (Eph. 1:18).

The most we can say is that death mars life. We can be frustrated that we will have to leave the people and things we love, and we miss those who have died already. But we can also rejoice that the best is yet to come and that death is just the door through which we must pass to completely enter into the joy of the Lord.

That is why a believer can be joyful in the face of death.

For the Christian, even death is a gracious gift from the loving Lord. It is not a tyrant. It is a servant to bring us into the joy of His presence. Completely. Forever.

Oppression

Oppression is a fact of life "under the sun." We would have to have our heads in the sand to miss it. Politically, we see it in the systematic violence of governments against their people. From the brutal tactics of the communist bloc to the shrill, frantic anti-communism of the oppressors in the rightist regimes, one reality remains consistent—oppression is a way of life in much of the world. "For the dark places of the earth are full of the habitations of cruelty" (Ps. 74:20, *NKJV*).

> Extortion turns a wise man into a fool, and a bribe corrupts the heart (Eccles. 7:7).

The person who oppresses others, or the one who accepts a bribe, is taking the first step along the path to ignominy. Oppression and bribery twist even a wise person's mind. Oppression destroys that which makes him wise in the first place and changes his heart so that he is accessible to bribes or vulnerable to flattery (which is the bribing of one's mind). It would be better to listen to the rebukes of friends than to be corrupted by dishonest praise.

On a personal level, we see the oppression of fathers and husbands who mistake responsibility for dictatorship, the abuse of children by cruel adults, and the exploitation of workers by their employers. There is plenty of this kind of misery in our world. Solomon talked about its influence in his world, too.

> Again I looked and saw all the oppression that was taking place under the sun: I saw the tears of the oppressed—and they have no comforter; power was on the side of their oppressors—and they have no comforter. And I declared that the dead, who had already died, are happier than the living, who are still

alive. But better than both is he who has not yet been, who has not seen the evil that is done under the sun (4:1-3).

"If you see the poor oppressed in a district, and justice and rights denied, do not be surprised at such things; for one official is eyed by a higher one, and over them both are others higher still. The increase from the land is taken by all; the king himself profits from the fields" (5:8,9).

Solomon does not dwell on this theme at length in Ecclesiastes. Perhaps that fact alone is mute testimony to the fact our world will never be completely free from oppression. There is little to say beyond observing the obvious fact: "power was on the side of their oppressors" (4:1). There always is. There is something about power that breeds the habit of oppression. It frequently corrupts those who possess it.

That may be the reason Solomon does not dwell on the benefits of revolution or reform. Tyranny seems to expand to fill the power available, and the level of oppression does not seem to subside as one regime replaces another. At the same time, however, one must admit that the level of oppression varies drastically from one nation to another. What might be viewed as oppression by many in the United States would be dearly welcomed relief in Cambodia.

Solomon paints with a wide brush when he declares that "they have no comforter" (4:1). He seems to be saying that no matter what we do to comfort the oppressed or work on their behalf, oppression will still exist. Oppressors soon become comfortable with their station in life.

In chapter 5, verses 8 and 9 offer an interesting explanation of how oppression maintains itself. Solomon describes how oppressors justify their actions. They do it by convincing themselves it is their duty, that they are just doing their job, as Adolph Eichmann described his role in sending hundreds of thousands of Jews to the gas chamber during World War II. Each official is preoccupied with his own little kingdom and turns a deaf ear to the suffering that takes place around him. Indeed, they are "eyed" by their own superiors; so even the officials are oppressed by those who lord it over them.

We should "not be surprised at such things" (5:8). No utopia is around the corner. Solomon knew it, and so do we! Anyone who lives in the world of business or politics knows that power is only power when there is no doubt that those who possess it are able and willing to use it.

When I first read verses 2 and 3 of chapter 4, I was taken back by their hopelessness.

> And I declared that the dead, who had already died,
> are happier than the living, who are still alive. But bet-
> ter than both is he who has not yet been, who has not
> seen the evil that is done under the sun (4:2,3).

Granted, I thought, oppression is terrible; but how could anyone really believe that those who were never born are the fortunate ones?

I now believe that Solomon was speaking of evil in its most systematic and cruel forms. We do not experience that sort of oppression in our country, so perhaps we are unqualified to understand how awful oppression is. On the other hand, it is possible that Solomon is employing hyperbole (a deliberate exaggeration for its literary effect) to shock us into facing the hideous evils we find it so easy to ignore.

The secular world has no answer to this unpleasant reality of life, this "vanity of vanities." Its appeals to reform or revolution end in disillusionment all too often.

God had an answer to oppression—His Son, Jesus.

Jesus experienced the brutal realities of life. His trial was a mockery of justice, and His death was as real as any death has ever been. He was oppressed.

> He was oppressed and afflicted, yet he did not open
> his mouth; he was led like a lamb to the slaughter, and
> as sheep before her shearers is silent, so he did not
> open his mouth. By oppression and judgment, he was
> taken away. And who can speak of his descendants?

For he was cut off from the land of the living; for the transgression of my people he was stricken (Isa. 53:7,8).

Jesus knew where His life was headed. He would die; He would live. And all injustice and oppression, and even death itself, would be defeated.

We are told to work at being peacemakers (Matt. 5:9). We are to feed the hungry, help the poor, visit widows and orphans, and perform many other acts of mercy and peacemaking. They all come with our calling as Christians. On one hand we work at correcting injustice and oppression, and on the other hand we realize that these evils will continue until God intervenes in history to establish His kingdom.

In the meantime, we live in the tension. Life's harsh side is real, but so is the kingdom of God.

Striving for Success

I first met Thomas ten years ago. Young, good-looking, enormously talented, he had strong Christian convictions and was highly regarded by nearly everyone. But he was also highly motivated to acquire wealth, and before long stories of his shady business dealings and immorality were whispered throughout the community. For a while it looked as if he was going to get by with it; he was smart and quick enough on his feet to pull it off if anyone could.

But then it fell apart. Business. Family. Friends. Eventually his ambitious drive for success began to destroy everything he valued.

The pursuit of success can be one of life's most disillusioning goals. By its nature, success is an elusive goal; and even when it is achieved, it can be frighteningly brief and fleeting. Solomon had seen the futility of striving for success, and he quickly came to the essence of the problem it poses. "And I saw that all labor and all achievement spring from man's envy of his neighbor. This too is meaningless, a chasing after the wind" (Eccles. 4:4).

Interestingly enough, the Hebrew allows for two meanings

for this verse. Our translation says we pursue success only because we are envious of others' accomplishments. Other translations suggest one person's success is a cause for envy by others.

Regardless, the basic point is still valid. All of us think highly of ourselves and want to stand above the crowd; we do not take kindly to being number two in anything. We want to outshine our neighbors, and we get into the rat race and beat our heads against the wall trying to outdo others.

Is this true of everybody and everything? Is this the only reason people strive to achieve? The word *all* is used in two ways in Scripture; it is used both as "all" in general and as "all" in particular. So when Solomon says, "All toil and every skillful work," most likely he is painting with his wide brush.

He is saying, "As I look at the world, I see that people are working themselves to death because they want to outshine their neighbors. They want to have more than someone else; they are envious, jealous." He is not necessarily saying that every action we take has this motive. He is saying that the sum ("all" in the general sense) of our efforts adds up to envy. It is vain, empty.

Solomon is not suggesting that we should not work hard or not do our work well. He is speaking of the person who has become immersed in "keeping up with the Joneses" and is working too hard. "I have seen that generally the person who is a workaholic is trying to prove something; he envies his neighbor and wants to get ahead of him."

Of course, there is the opposite extreme. I might add that the fact that Solomon wrote about the lazy individual in the next verse shows he does not mean "all" literally in verse 4. "The fool folds his hands and ruins himself" (4:5).

The lazy man is a fool. When Solomon says that he "consumes his own flesh" (as the *NKJV* translates it), he means that he eats what he already has. He looks at the overachiever and says, "Man, that's not for me. I'm just going to sit around and take what's given to me and live off what I already have." So he eats his seed corn.

This man reminds us of the wealthy farmer of Jesus' parable.

The farmer, too, decided that he could live off what he owned, choosing to "eat, drink and be merry" (Luke 12:19). Jesus referred to this man as a fool, as Solomon had done centuries earlier when he wrote this passage.

If the workaholic and the drop-out are inadequate role models, what is the answer?

> Better one handful with tranquillity than two handfuls
> with toil and chasing after the wind (Eccles. 4:6).

Solomon says, "Rather than grasping for so much that you have to be a workaholic to get it, be content with less. It is better to have less but enjoy it more."

Our problem is less the high cost of living than it is the cost of high living. We want too much. Solomon says we should scale down our expectations.

A friend recently told me of a visitor from a foreign country who was taken to see one of our large department stores. After a few minutes' time, the man rather incredulously said, "Look at all the things I don't need." First Timothy says, "Godliness with contentment is great gain . . . . People who want to get rich fall into temptation and a trap" (6:6,9).

We are to keep our lives in balance. We ought not work so hard to fill both fists. The truth is that our wants will always exceed our grasp anyway, even when we grasp with both fists! Solomon is pleading for a balanced life in which we work as God wants us to work and take what He gives, instead of striving for more.

Solomon has commented on this idea in other places:

> Better a little with the fear of the Lord than great
> wealth with turmoil. Better a meal of vegetables
> where there is love than a fattened calf with hatred
> . . . . Better a little with righteousness than much gain
> with injustice (Prov. 15:16,17; 16:8).

Many homes would be better off working at nurturing love,

rather than searching for success. No meal tastes very good without love, but even a meager meal can be good when love is present. And no amount of financial success gained through injustice will ever be as good as less gained righteously. It is a poor life, indeed, that is impoverished in every area except wealth.

But there is more to be considered. Solomon is not finished with this subject.

The Folly of Materialism

Again I saw something meaningless under the sun:
There was a man all alone; he had neither son nor
brother. There was no end to his toil, yet his eyes
were not content with his wealth. "For whom am I
toiling," he asked, "and why am I depriving myself of
enjoyment?" This too is meaningless—a miserable
business! (Eccles. 4:7,8).

In order to illustrate the folly of materialistic living, Solomon describes someone who is concerned with success but never asks himself why he is working so hard. Earlier in the book Solomon pointed out that we do not know who will benefit from our work (see 2:18) or whether they will be wise or foolish (see 2:19). But here he is looking at the problem, What shall I do with success, from a different point of view.

This man has no son or brother—a poetic way of saying he is alone. He has nobody who cares for him or to whom he can leave his wealth. With his single-minded devotion to gain (which Solomon has already assured us he cannot keep for himself), this man probably has no friends, either. He is too busy for friends or family; and as he pursues success after pointless success, he never asks, "For whom do I toil? Why do I deny myself of good?" (see 4:8).

These verses could describe a person who does have a home, wife, and children as easily as not. The truth is that this man's heart is where his treasure is (see Matt. 6:21). If he were to have family and friends, he would not have them for long. He would sacrifice them on the altar of his drive for success.

So even the pursuit of success is meaningless. It is vain. Pointless.

Companionship

Solomon moves from the subject of success at any cost, a philosophy that leads one to be alone and empty, to the subject of companionship. In this section he talks about how much better it is to have companions in life, whether in marriage or in friendships.

> Two are better than one, because they have a good
> return for their work: If one falls down, his friend can
> help him up. But pity the man who falls and has no one
> to help him up! Also, if two lie down together, they
> will keep warm. But how can one keep warm alone?
> Though one may be overpowered, two can defend
> themselves. A cord of three strands is not quickly bro-
> ken (Eccles. 4:9-12).

Solomon gives four rewards of companionship in these verses. The first is that companions can get more done: "Two are better than one, because they have a good return for their work" (v. 9).

Second, good companions know you well enough to know your faults: "If one falls down, his friend can help him up. But pity the man who falls and has no one to help him up!" (v. 10). It is good to have someone who knows our faults. That person can help us through the times when we fail and do not know why; he or she can help us do better next time.

I think it strange that we sometimes become defensive in our close relationships. If someone criticizes us, we think we have failed and that the person suddenly dislikes us. But one of the *chief* values of our being intimate with someone is so we can learn when we are wrong. "Faithful are the wounds of a friend" (Prov. 27:6). We ought to be thankful when someone who knows and loves us corrects our errors. A companion, one who knows our sins and weaknesses and is willing to help us overcome them, is part of God's provision for us.

The third reward of good companionship is warmth. "Also, if two lie down together, they will keep warm. But how can one keep warm alone?" (v. 11). There is the obvious physical side to this advantage. However, I think Solomon is also talking about emotional warmth. Every society has had its ways to find physical warmth, and the rich (which is the context of his discussion) in every time and place have the least problem with cold weather. When we live our lives alone, we live in a cold world. All of us need somebody somewhere—a spouse, a good friend, a counselor.

The fourth value of companionship is strength. "Though one may be overpowered, two can defend themselves. A cord of three strands is not quickly broken" (v. 12). Solomon is suggesting that we might get in trouble some day; if that happens, we will be better off if we have someone who stands with us as our strength.

Solomon's final statement is interesting. "A cord of three strands is not quickly broken" (v. 12). There is no single illustration that can convey all that statement means. It does illustrate how the love of a man and a woman can be strengthened when a child is born into their family. In view of Solomon's interest in pointing out how desperately we need God in our lives, I believe we should understand the expression to indicate that when God is involved in a relationship, it "is not quickly broken." That is, where God is *allowed* to be God in a marriage, it does not become broken. It might if He is there but has been put on the shelf. This principle holds true in all our relationships.

There are two reasons for making an issue of this. First, we must not try to go through life alone. Whether we are married or single, have loads of friends or few, we need one another. Christians of all ages need the support of other Christians. I recommend that every Christian become a part of a support group; I have benefited from one for many years. We get together to share our joys and our burdens, and we stay in touch with one another to be sure we do not let anyone down.

The second reason for making this an issue is that we need to see there is a price to pay for lasting companionship. Verse 9 uses the word *better*, in fact, Solomon uses it 21 times in Ecclesiastes. It is "better" to have companionship; most of us would agree with that. But we must be prepared to pay the price for good friends and good marriages.

When we enter into marriage or make friends or develop a close relationship with other Christians, we lose our independence. We joke when a friend is about to marry, "Oh, you're going to bite the dust. Marriage is a ball . . . and chain!" However, there is a touch of truth to this joking. If we try to keep our independence and enter into marriage, we will not have a good marriage. If we think we do not have to take the ideas or feelings or needs of others into consideration, we will not have true companionship—or friendship—with them. "In humility consider others better than yourselves. Each of you should look not only to your own interests, but also to the interests of others" (Phil. 2:3,4).

Whether it is in marriage, friendship, or the church, we have to be ready to listen to others ("This person's ideas might be better than mine"), ready to learn their interests ("There might be something good for me in it"), ready to look out for their needs ("I am God's neighbor for this person"), ready to adjust to their pace and style ("Two of us cannot walk together if we walk at different speeds").

Yes, companionship is better, but there is a price, and it must be paid every day. Is it worth it? You bet! But we must not forget the price, or it will no longer be good.

Leadership

Being a king, Solomon had ample opportunity to think about leadership, especially in the political realm.

"Better a poor but wise youth than an old but foolish king who no longer knows how to take warning. The youth may have come from prison to the kingship, or he may have been born in poverty within his kingdom. I saw that all who lived and walked under the sun followed the youth, the king's successor. There was no end to all the people who were before them. But those who came later were not pleased with the successor. This too is meaningless, a chasing after the wind" (Eccles. 4:13-16).

Solomon had seen the comings and goings of leaders. Even his own experience had taught him that popularity is frequently short-lived; that which endears a leader to the masses can alienate them from him just as quickly.

Solomon seems to be comparing two kinds of kings. One has been on the throne a long time. Regardless of whether he ruled well in his earlier years, he has become so accustomed to power that he forgets that he needs advice. He becomes a poor leader. Then a young man comes along, only this young man built his support at the grass roots level. Suddenly, everyone is following the new king and the old one is replaced. This certainly sounds "better" (v. 13). But wait! "But those who came later were not pleased with the successor" (v. 16). The next generation will reject him. So it goes with leadership.

In the Introduction we noted that one of Solomon's key points in Ecclesiastes is that nothing is permanent. Here he gives us another illustration of life's impermanence. Who, after all, has more security than a king? He has all the power of a kingdom at his disposal. And yet, in this illogical world in which we live, even the people who should be able to control events are unable to do so. They, too, become victims of life's fickle fortunes.

Time and familiarity have a way of eroding popularity. Not many leaders stay at the top for long. Politically, most of the recent presidents of the United States were acclaimed when they were elected but fell out of favor before their terms were half-completed. Few managers of major league teams or coaches of the top college teams stay at their jobs throughout their careers. The people who shouted "Hosanna" to Jesus also called for His crucifixion.

Both of the kings Solomon presents came to the same end. Popular acclaim does not last, and those who aspire to positions of leadership would be wise to remember that. It does not seem to make a great deal of difference whether one is a good ruler or not; those who come along later will not be pleased with him either.

This does not have to be as pessimistic as it sounds. Remember, Solomon is addressing his words to one who chooses to live his life without considering how God relates to it. He is pointing out what any fair-minded person can observe for himself. What Solomon wants his secular-minded friend—and us—to see is that even at its highest levels, life is insecure. We cannot depend upon anything that is of this world. And if our highest dreams turn out to be nightmares when God is not a part of them, what, then, should those of us who do not enjoy positions of power, popularity, and acclaim expect?

Leadership—power, money, influence, acclaim—is not where satisfaction is to be found. One cannot depend on leadership, anymore than one can depend on any other form of worldly success. Only the One who gives these gifts will not fail us. He is satisfying and permanent. In Him there is no vanity; indeed, in Him there is a great profit, great gain.

Questions for Discussion

1. Are you, like Solomon, disheartened at the injustices of this world? What have you done recently to alleviate injustice in your own corner of the world? What is the extent of the believer's responsibility? (E.g. verses in Psalms and Proverbs regarding the poor.)
2. How has God made even death "beautiful in its time" in your life?
3. Do you agree with Solomon that "all labor and all achievement spring from man's envy of his neighbor" (Eccles. 4:4)? Why? Why not? From what perspective was he writing?
4. Read Solomon's description of companionship in Ecclesiastes 4:9-12. How well does Solomon's description describe your relationships with friends and loved ones? How can you increase godly intimacy with others?

CHAPTER FIVE

Be Real When You Worship

Ecclesiastes 5:1-9

On the surface, it is hard to imagine how worship, of all things, could be "vain"—empty and worthless. Yet that is the picture Solomon paints in this section of Ecclesiastes, that of worship gone to seed and now become empty and worthless. This worship is "vain" because of the insincerity with which it is offered and by the thoughtlessness by which it is motivated. It was a problem in Solomon's time; it is with us today.

How many times I have heard people say they do not attend any church because it is not meaningful to them. I believe people when they tell me that. Obviously, if worship had meant much to them, they would have continued. Ironically, we get out of worship what we invest in it; and even the best preacher in the world cannot "feed" people who come to the hour of worship with closed mouths!

But not everyone who finds worship to be empty of meaning drops out of the church. Some keep coming, regularly or irregularly, for whatever reasons. They are the people to whom Solomon addressed these remarks. He was concerned by the problems created by empty worship, and in looking around himself he realized it was rooted in the very reason one worships. Does one worship God because He is the Holy One who ought to be loved and praised? Does one worship God for the emotional thrill of warmth or ecstasy that comes from being in His presence? Does one worship God in order to be seen worshiping God?

As Solomon looked around, he realized that the problem of the secular mind was not confined to people who lived as though God were unimportant in their lives. Many of the people who worshiped regularly at the Temple were equally secular in their approach to God. They were worshiping themselves, not God. They were making a joke out of worship.

So Solomon protested, "Your worship is a farce. It is an exercise in futility. You drag your body to worship, but your mind is in another world. You listen with half an ear, you sing half-heartedly, and you plan out your next week's work while the Word of God is being taught. You give nothing to God when you worship. You expect nothing. And that is what you get—nothing!"

Because Solomon understood the human heart so well, he suggested several steps we can take to insure that our worship is fresh and meaningful. Interestingly enough, he listed them in chronological order—before, during, and after the worship hour.

I believe he handled the subject this way because he knew that our failure to worship God properly is rooted in our being unprepared to worship, our lack of attention to what is happening during worship, and our inability or unwillingness to follow through on our commitments once we leave the sanctuary.

Before Worship

Guard your steps when you go to the house of God (Eccles. 5:1).

Solomon was thinking of the Temple in Jerusalem when he wrote of "the house of God." It was the place where Israel worshiped God; when we worship with other Christians, we normally worship at the church. Regardless, we can also worship God by ourselves in our "room," as Jesus said (Matt. 6:6).

Solomon says, "Walk prudently. Guard your steps." We

should give our minds to our worship long before we arrive at the place for worship. We ought to prepare ourselves so that when we arrive, our worship will be deliberate, grateful, and heartfelt.

The Gospel of John says, "Yet a time is coming and has now come when the true worshipers will worship the Father in spirit and truth, for they are the kind of worshipers the Father seeks" (John 4:23). God is delighted when we worship Him; but He is offended when our worship is casual or haphazard.

There are several examples of careless worship mentioned in the Bible. In Leviticus 15 God warns the Israelites not to come to the Tabernacle to worship when they are unclean and have not prepared themselves, "so they will not die in their uncleanness for defiling my dwelling place" (Lev. 15:31).

In Hebrews chapter 10 it says that in preparing a place in heaven for us and in preparing us to worship Him there, God went to the extreme of giving His Son in death so that we could "enter the Most Holy Place by the blood of Jesus" (v. 19). God's holiness demands that we prepare ourselves to worship and that we do not take it casually. If our worship is going to be authentic and fruitful, it must begin before we arrive.

There are a number of steps we can take in preparation for our worship of God. First, we can anticipate the hour. We ought to cultivate an anticipation for worship. If Jesus Christ is really our Lord and He means more to us than anything else, then we should come to this hour with anticipation. The hour when we worship together should be the high point of our week.

Second, we ought to pray for the hour of worship. We ought to be in intercessory prayer throughout the week, but we ought to approach the hour of worship with two prayers in mind. We ought to pray, "Speak to each person in this service, Lord" and "Speak to me first."

If we do not prepare our hearts for worship, we might not worship God "in spirit and truth" (John 4:23), and we might cheat ourselves of a meaningful encounter with the Lord. When we do not "get much out of it" during worship, it almost always is due to our failure to prepare our hearts. Even the heaviest rain will run off parched, hard ground. We will miss the blessings of God when our hearts are not soft and pliable, and we need to prepare ourselves for worship with prayer.

It is interesting that some people get a lot from every worship experience, while others seldom appreciate the privilege they have of worshiping the Lord. Why is it that one person is moved by God during a worship service, while another complains about not being fed? Is it a matter of being prepared? Does it come from confusing worship with entertainment? We should be able to worship God and have a fresh encounter with Him even if the organ is broken, the pastor has laryngitis, and the choir is on vacation!

Third, we need to prepare ourselves physically. Perhaps I am more aware of this because I am a pastor and often preach three times on Sunday, but I do not know how someone who is physically exhausted on Sunday morning can thoroughly enter into a worship of God in mind, in body, or in spirit. We need to be sure we are not physically exhausted, emotionally distracted, or mentally preoccupied with events in our lives. We should also be prudent about how we spend our Saturday evenings.

We want to be ready to worship God.

During Worship

Solomon has some strong words for the person who has come to worship in a casual fashion.

> Go near to listen rather than to offer the sacrifice of
> fools, who do not know that they do wrong. Do not be
> quick with your mouth, do not be hasty in your heart
> to utter anything before God. God is in heaven and
> you are on earth, so let your words be few. As a
> dream comes when there are many cares, so the
> speech of a fool when there are many words (Eccles.
> 5:1-3).

"Go near to listen" means: "Come with open, tender hearts. Come with listening ears. Don't come to tell God what to do." We can tell God what we want, but we must come near to listen

to Him. That is better than to offer "the sacrifice of fools" (v. 1).
The sacrifice of fools is empty words. The fool has forgotten
both who God is and who he himself is. He takes liberties with
the grace and patience of God. A fool is such a fool that he does
not know that what he is doing is evil (see v. 1).

What is it that a fool does when he "worships"? We have to
look at what Solomon tells us *not* to do to see what the fool was
doing: "Do not be quick with your mouth, do not be hasty in your
heart to utter anything before God. God is in heaven and you are
on earth, so let your words be few" (v. 2). There is a big difference between God and us. The fool forgets that difference when
he worships. He is hasty with his words, not thinking them
through or praying them with sincerity.

When Solomon says, "let your words be few," he is not
speaking so much about long prayers as about pretentious praying. God cannot stand our pouring out empty phrases in worship, but He does honor persistent prayer (see Luke 11:5-8).

In Genesis 32:22-29 we read of Jacob's wrestling with God
and declaring that he would not let go until God blessed him. And
God blessed him. God is not against long or persistent prayers if
they mean something to the one raising them. He wants us to
spend much time in prayer with Him, but He does not want
empty, vain words that do not come from the heart.

We know how that is. When we talk with someone whose
mind is somewhere else and the whole conversation becomes an
extended vocalized pause, we may be insulted. We excuse ourselves as quickly as we can. This kind of verbal doodling irritates
us. It irritates God, too. He wants sincere prayers.

Solomon has already discussed the fool in Ecclesiastes (2:14-
16,19; 4:5,13), and he will return to it again later (6:8;
7:6,17,25; 10:2,3,12,14,15). Nowhere does he speak more
directly about the consequence of being a fool than here: the fool
does his folly naturally. "A fool's voice is known by his many
words" (5:3, *NKJV*). He cannot help himself.

When Solomon compares foolish worship with a dream-filled
night, he touches on something most people understand. Nearly
everyone has had hectic days when there was so much happening that the night was filled with tossing and turning and strange

dreams. I know one man who cannot sleep for hours after going to an exciting basketball game, even though it has been nearly twenty years since he has played in a serious game himself.

There is something about us that makes it hard for us to shut off our minds after a hectic or exciting day, and so we dream dreams. It happens naturally. Just as a busy day causes dreams, so a fool causes empty words. Where you have one, you have the other. We ought not play the fool in our worship.

After Worship

How many times I have heard someone castigate the hypocrites in the church! Where else would we like to see them? The hypocrites *should* be at church. However, hypocrisy is a serious issue in the church; probably most Christians have heard more on this subject than we care to hear. Solomon had something important to say about hypocritical worship. "When you make a vow to God, do not delay in fulfilling it. He has no pleasure in fools; fulfill your vow. It is better not to vow than to make a vow and not fulfill it" (5:4,5).

I like the way Solomon understands us. He does not say, "*If* you make a vow to God." He says, "*When* you make a vow to God." We all make vows, or commitments. Solomon understood that. He also knew that we need to be as prompt in keeping our vows as we are in making them.

We are not to delay in paying our vows. *Delay* is the key word here. No one makes a vow with the intention of breaking it, but it is easy to make our vows, walk out of the place of worship, and set them aside, assuming we will fulfill them later. But all too easily tomorrow becomes next week, and next week becomes next month, and next month becomes next year—or never. The consequence is that many Christians live defeated lives because they made vows to God and have not kept them.

In another place Solomon wrote, "It is a trap for a man to dedicate something rashly and only later to consider his vows" (Prov. 20:25). It is easy to make a vow in a sincere moment and then avoid it once we have had time to consider its cost.

It is interesting that even early in Israel's history, allowance had been made for this human weakness. In Deuteronomy it is written: "But if you refrain from making a vow, you will not be guilty. Whatever your lips utter you must be sure to do, because you made your vow freely to the Lord your God with your own mouth" (Deut. 23:22,23). We would be better off not to make any vows than to make them and look for excuses to avoid them.

There is a story in the New Testament that describes an incident that happened in the early church. Ananias and Sapphira sold some property, apparently to keep a vow they had made; but when the time came to pay it, they withheld part of it but presented the rest as if it were the entire amount they had received. They both were struck dead by the Lord because they withheld what they pretended to give to the Lord (see Acts 5:1-11). It is a serious business when we make vows to God, and we ought not make them lightly.

Nothing hardens a heart or sears a conscience as much as being brought to the point of melting and then cooling to the same old shape. "It is better not to vow than to make a vow and not fulfill it. Do not let your mouth lead you into sin. And do not protest to the temple messenger, 'My vow was a mistake.' Why should God be angry at what you say and destroy the work of your hands? Much dreaming and many words are meaningless. Therefore stand in awe of God" (Eccles. 5:5-7).

The people who make Christian plaques should make one of "Do not let your mouth lead you into sin" (v. 6). I can think of many applications for that statement, but its context is the vow we have made. We ought not to let ourselves sin in making our commitments to the Lord by trying to excuse ourselves from keeping them. "Oh, that was a mistake, Lord. I really shouldn't have made that vow." We ought not try to escape our vows.

The tragic breakdown of marriages in our time is an illustration of our hypocritical worship. Marriage is a covenant; both partners take vows before God to keep that covenant (see Mal. 2:14). To break one's marriage covenant is to break a vow made before God as surely as is failing to give Him the gift we have promised.

It is a serious business to avoid our vows to the Lord. The question "Why should God be angry at what you say and destroy the work of your hands?" (Eccles. 5:6) presents frightening possibilities. The costs of not keeping our vows may become greater than the costs of paying them. This, too, is vanity.

We are not to dream about what we are going to do; we are to do it (see v. 7). If we never make any commitments to the Lord, we are not going to grow with Him. We need to make our commitments. But they should be sober, deliberate, thoughtful, reverent. And we should keep them so that our worship does not become just one more vanity in a vain world!

It is a great privilege we have to worship God. It is also a serious business. We ought to come with hearts that are prepared. We ought to be sober in the commitments we make. We ought to do what we promise God we will do. This is what God expects from true worship.

It will give us great joy when we offer it to Him!

Questions for Discussion

1. What religious practices do you find to be empty or meaningless in your life? Which are most meaningful? What steps can you take to make the "empty" aspects of your relationship with God more meaningful?
2. What steps do you take on Saturday night and early Sunday morning to ready yourself for worship? How can you improve your preparation for worshiping God?
3. What steps can you take to help you concentrate on glorifying God instead of concentrating on the worries and problems that often distract during worship?
4. Have you made a vow before the Lord recently? What actions are you taking to fulfill it?

CHAPTER SIX

The Limited Value of Wealth

Ecclesiastes 5:10–6:12

One of Solomon's first statements in Ecclesiastes was, "What does man gain from all his labor?" (1:3). It should not surprise us, then, that eventually he would talk about profit and its pursuit. Centuries later, the apostle Paul would declare, "For the love of money is a root of all kinds of evil. Some people, eager for money, have wandered from the faith and pierced themselves with many griefs (1 Tim. 6:10).

Money, and the love of it, is a basic motivation of life "under the sun," that is, in the observable world. It is no accident that when the obviously successful person on the television screen discreetly leans toward a friend and says, "My broker is E. F. Hutton, and E. F. Hutton says . . . " everyone drops whatever he or she is doing to eavesdrop.

Profit is important to us. We crave it. Sometimes we even live and die for it.

Solomon was the wisest man who had ever lived (see 1 Kings 4:29-34). He would not have had to have been all that wise, though, to know that men and women crave wealth. He knew that many people live for wealth; but his wisdom helped him see that most of us do not realize how little happiness and satisfaction it will bring us. So he challenges his readers to take an honest look at the meaninglessness (the vanity) of riches.

The Unsatisfactory Nature of Wealth

The irony of wealth is that it is not necessary to have a lot of money to love it. Some people believe "the vanity of riches" refers to rich people. Yet, it may or may not refer to the rich. When we talk about the love of money, we are talking about people at every level of income. Some of the world's most materialistic people do not have two nickels to rub together. And frankly, some of the wealthy people I know seem to hold it very loosely and do not appear to be preoccupied with money.

In talking about the love of money, we are not talking about people of any particular economic level. However, we need to remember that as our goods increase, we are probably in greater danger of growing attached to them or of selfishly striving to attain more regardless of the cost. It is important that we do not allow money to become a substitute for God in our lives or try to make it do something it will never be able to do.

It is "profitable" for us to understand the true value of wealth. We can be grateful that Solomon gave us several insights into its nature. In doing so, he proclaims that living for wealth is unsatisfying and self-defeating. There are several reasons why this is true.

We Always Want More

1. *The more we gain, the more we desire.* The pursuit of wealth is much like an addiction. It feeds on itself and will consume the person who is not careful.

> Whoever loves money never has money enough; whoever loves wealth is never satisfied with his income.
> This too is meaningless (Eccles. 5:10).

Solomon has observed something nearly everyone can see. When materials things are the focus of life, our desires always outrun our ability to acquire or to enjoy. I am told that someone once asked John D. Rockefeller, "How much money do you want?" Mr. Rockefeller answered, "Just a little bit more." That is how it is with wealth. No matter how much we have, we want just a little bit more.

I live in the midst of a fast moving, materialistic city. I see the emptiness that living for wealth can bring. Of course, I also know some wealthy people whose lives radiate joy and happiness. One of the big differences is in the importance they attach to their wealth. That is why both the wealthy and the poor can suffer equally from the love-of-money disease.

It works like this: God has placed eternity within our hearts (see 3:11). This means that at the core of who we are, God has planted a hunger for the eternal that nothing else can satisfy. So when we substitute anything for God (the Bible calls this sin by its name—idolatry), we create a dangerous imbalance in our lives. We become unfocused. Because of the way God made us, underneath everything we have a great hunger for Him. However, we are easily confused by the temptation to put something else at the center; in this case that temptation is money. That is why we become unhappy whenever money becomes too important; we become out of focus with what God created us to be. Instead of the gain which the love of money promises, we are left with emptiness!

A life built on the pursuit of wealth will not bring satisfaction, no matter how much a person obtains. It is vanity. It is empty.

The More We Have, the More We Spend

2. *Our expenses keep up with our income.* Notice how Solomon describes the fate of the person who becomes financially successful:

> As goods increase, so do those who consume them.
> And what benefit are they to the owner except to
> feast his eyes on them? (5:11).

As our wealth increases, so do the people who try to get

their fingers in our pie! There is an interesting passage in Isaiah that illustrates this principle. A man named Eliakim is promised that he will become an important official, but he is warned that the hangers-on will become a terrible burden. Picturing him as a peg on a wall, Isaiah declares: "All the glory of his family will hang on him: its offspring and offshoots—all its lesser vessels, from the bowls to all the jars" (22:24). His success would be a burden instead of a joy.

One of the frustrations that comes with financial success is that we then need people to manage and protect our wealth. We need lawyers and accountants and managers and experts of all sorts. We also attract the very people who will take our wealth away from us if we let them! That is one of the reasons we need the counsel of yet even more experts.

So Solomon looks at all this and asks an interesting question: Is it really worth the effort? If wealth brings the parasites out of the woodwork, and if we will need assistance to manage what we have, what's the point of having it? What good is it, other than to watch it as it slips through our fingers?

Earlier, Solomon had pointed out the futility of achievement: no matter how successful we are, we will not be remembered (see Eccles. 2:16) and someone else will enjoy what we have built (see 2:21). Here he says that the truth is even worse than that: wealth will bring us burdens, and we will not gain nearly as much as we think we will. Other than the enjoyment of watching it come and go, there is not much gain, only prestige. The hangers-on will do their best to eat us out of house and home.

Additional Wealth Means
Additional Worry

3. *Wealth may bring sleepless nights.* I am amazed at how many people cannot sleep at night because of tension. They have so many responsibilities, or they are working so hard to become successful, or they are so worried about the future that they cannot sleep. Wealth, especially our concern for it, often results in insomnia.

> The sleep of a laborer is sweet, whether he eats little
> or much, but the abundance of a rich man permits him
> no sleep (5:12).

The laboring man may not bring home a large paycheck, but he works hard and his sleep is sweet. Why? The first reason is that he has worked hard and his body is tired. The second is that he has little cause for worry. He does not have to worry about what the stock market will look like in the morning, and he does not have to worry about keeping his subordinates productive and the business profitable. He had a job to do, and he did it. At the end of the day he ate whatever food he could and slept peacefully.

The wealthy man did not enjoy the same rest. His sleeplessness is not the insomnia that comes from too much work to do (see 2:23). Rather, because he has more than he needs, he is able to indulge himself and is more likely to eat and drink too much and do too little physical work. The fact that his wealth brings him greater burdens does not help him, either. As a result, he has trouble sleeping and tosses and turns throughout the night (see 5:12).

We understand what Solomon means when he talks about too much food and too little physical exercise. He could easily be describing our culture. It is no wonder we find it necessary to join health clubs and fitness centers to undo the damages of our prosperous, sedentary lives.

Wealth Doesn't Guarantee Security

4. *Our wealth may vanish.*

> I have seen a grievous evil under the sun: wealth
> hoarded to the harm of its owner, or wealth lost
> through some misfortune, so that when he has a son
> there is nothing left for him (5:13,14).

It is possible that Solomon is talking about a miserly use of wealth, but I think instead that he is referring to a business venture that went sour. The word translated "misfortune" in verse 14 is the same word that obviously refers to work or burden in other verses in Ecclesiastes (e.g., 1:13, 3:10; 8:16). Solomon's point is that the businessman's venture went so bad that at the end of his life he had "no gain" to give to his heir.

This man had two problems. First, he was broke. This was bad enough. But the tragedy is that he had toiled and had been vexed (see 5:17) the entire time he was creating his wealth (like the man in 2:23). His work created so much pressure for him that he was miserable while he gained his wealth. The irony is that his life was ruined twice over, once in gaining his wealth and again in losing it.

We all have known or heard of people whose wealth has evaporated almost overnight. Earlier in my ministry a man came to me with that very story. He had been wealthy, but had lost every penny he had. The possibility that wealth might vanish is always present, and that is one of the simple realities of this world that makes the love of wealth an unwise, unsatisfying base upon which to build our lives.

Solomon has one more observation to make about the unsatisfactory nature of riches.

Trust in God, Not Riches

5. *We cannot take our wealth with us.* We know this, but we are quick to forget it.

> Naked a man comes from his mother's womb, and as
> he comes, so he departs. He takes nothing from his
> labor that he can carry in his hand. This too is a griev-
> ous evil: As a man comes, so he departs, and what
> does he gain, since he toils for the wind? All his days
> he eats in darkness, with great frustration, affliction
> and anger (5:15-17).

There is no need to overwork the point. When my life is over, exactly what will I take away with me?

Nothing.

Solomon uses a clever phrase in verse 16. He asks, "And

what does he gain, since he toils for the wind?" Earlier in Ecclesiastes he has commented that he has "seen all the things that are done under the sun; all of them are meaningless, a chasing after the wind" (1:14). Now he says that we have even *worked* "for the wind."

To work for wealth is like working for the wind. Just as you get it, you lose it. It is gone, like a vapor, a puff. Regardless of whether one ever suffers the losses described in verses 13 and 14 and regardless of whether one ever amasses a fortune, in the end we have nothing material to show for our lives.

Where we are going we can take nothing with us.

So why should we live like the miser? Why "eat in darkness"? (This may be a figure of speech for the gloom of a miserable life lived for riches only.) Why fill our lives with "frustration, affliction and anger" by striving for a wealth that we will ultimately lose anyway?

This is a serious question. It cuts across every economic level, and it points to the basic futility of a life lived for wealth, "for the wind." It is vanity. It is miserable lot. Vanity of vanities!

It would be better to remember the words of the apostle Paul to Timothy: "Command those who are rich in this present world not to be arrogant nor to put their hope in wealth, which is so uncertain, but to put their hope in God, who richly provides us with everything for our enjoyment" (1 Tim. 6:17). Solomon has more to say on this subject and moves on to declare where we can find satisfaction and joy.

Satisfaction Is a Gift from God

Many years ago, I ran across an article written by an older pastor whom I have known most of my adult life. In reflecting upon his life, he wrote, "If I had my ministry to do over again, I would seek to enjoy it more." We are to enjoy our lives, not to seek wealth. Solomon expressed it this way: "Then I realized that it is good and proper for a man to eat and drink, and to find satisfaction in his toilsome labor under the sun during the few days of life God has given him—for this is his lot. Moreover, when God gives any man wealth and possessions, and enables

him to enjoy them, to accept his lot and be happy in his work—
this is a gift of God. He seldom reflects on the days of his life,
because God keeps him occupied with gladness of heart"
(Eccles. 5:18-20).

Here, Solomon begins to give his prescription for achieving
satisfaction. At first it seems as if he is simply advocating a
return to a simple life-style of enjoying the good things in life.
But then Solomon introduces the key to our search for satisfaction—God. God gives what we need—food, drink, wealth, joy.
All of this "is a gift of God" (5:19). The *Revised Standard Version*
reminds us that God gives us the "power" to enjoy them. God is
both the satisfaction we seek and the source of all the good we
enjoy.

Solomon has been conducting an experiment in this book. He
is asking the secular-minded individual to look at life honestly
and consider the ultimate implications of his own philosophy.
Occasionally, Solomon lets his own beliefs come through
strongly, and this is one of those places. He is not content to
report vividly what everyone can see; he decides to give us a
glimpse of what God has shown him.

Solomon has decided that no matter what happens, he is
going to be grateful. He is going to enjoy his work (being a king
sounds like a pretty great job, anyway!). He is going to enjoy his
food; he is going to enjoy his relaxation—he is going to enjoy
everything. It is important to realize that he is speaking here as
a person of faith; he is showing the reader the principles by
which he lives and the reader should live. He has already warned
us that the pursuit of wealth will not make us happy. Now he tells
us simply to enjoy life.

It is a comfort to know that the ability to enjoy life is a gift
from God (see 5:19). We do not just decide to enjoy life and then
sit back and do it. Thus, he repeats the message of chapter 2:
"To the man who pleases him, God gives wisdom, knowledge
and happiness" (2:26). Happiness is God's gift.

Solomon's summary of the situation is beautiful. He says that
the person who loves God and puts the values of His kingdom
first will not be discouraged upon discovering that wealth will not
bring happiness; he already knows it. He has already found hap-

piness. God will keep him busy with the true desires of his heart. There is a surprise in all this, though—the desire of his heart is to know and love and serve God. His heart's desire is not to pursue something that is a poor substitute for the real thing.

Solomon has not finished with the subject of wealth. He continues to discuss it in terms of its uncertainties, its unknowns. He says, "We don't know enough to know if wealth will be good for us." Far too many of us crave wealth and assume its possession will make us happy and fulfilled. "Not necessarily so," says Solomon. He goes on to discuss three questions about wealth that none of us can answer.

Who Knows Whether We Will Enjoy Wealth?

In verse 19 of Ecclesiastes 5 we are told that the "power" to enjoy God's gifts is itself a gift. Here we begin to realize that this power might not be given to us. There are so many unknowns in life; and Solomon invites his secular-minded reader—and all who read his book—to look at this question carefully.

"I have seen another evil under the sun, and it weighs heavily on men: God gives a man wealth, possessions and honor, so that he lacks nothing his heart desires, but God does not enable him to enjoy them, and a stranger enjoys them instead. This is meaningless, a grievous evil. A man may have a hundred children and live many years; yet no matter how long he lives, if he cannot enjoy his prosperity and does not receive proper burial, I say that a stillborn child is better off than he. It comes without meaning, it departs in darkness, and in darkness its name is shrouded. Though it never saw the sun or knew anything, it has more rest than does that man—even if he lives a thousand years twice over but fails to enjoy his prosperity. Do not all go to the same place?" (6:1-6).

Earlier in Ecclesiastes Solomon wrote: "A man can do nothing better than to eat and drink and find satisfaction in his work. This too, I see, is from the hand of God" (2:24). He continues in verse 25 with "for without him, who can eat or find enjoyment?" If God does not give us the ability to enjoy life, we will be unable to enjoy it. Later, he also wrote: "That every man may eat and drink, and find satisfaction in all his toil—this is the gift of God" (3:13). Again he tells us that God wants us to enjoy life.

In chapter 5 Solomon repeats his assertion: "Then I realized that it is good and proper for a man to eat and drink, and to find satisfaction in his toilsome labor under the sun during the few days of life God has given him—for this is his lot" (5:18).

What Solomon wants to communicate is clear: God wants us to enjoy life. He wants us to enjoy the material things we possess. They are for our pleasure and joy.

Will we? Nobody knows for sure.

"I have seen another evil under the sun, and it weighs heavily on men: God gives a man wealth, possessions and honor, so that he lacks nothing his heart desires, but God does not enable him to enjoy them, and a stranger enjoys them instead. This is meaningless, a grievous evil" (6:1,2). The evil is that even though God has given this man the power to own these possessions, He has not given him the power to enjoy them. The cause for this failure could be war, sickness, oppression, or whatever. Regardless, God has not allowed him to enjoy his riches. Surely this is a "vain" and "evil affliction" to the heart of one whose vision is limited to this life only.

Following this, Solomon lists some of the things, other than wealth, that have great value to people. "A man may have a hundred children" (in those days a hundred children would have been considered a great joy; they were an economic asset to the family) "and live many years; yet no matter how long he lives," (in verse 6 he says that even if you live "a thousand years twice over"—two thousand years!) "if he cannot enjoy his prosperity and does not receive proper burial," (in those days the manner in which you were buried was a statement about the significance of your life) "a stillborn child is better off than he" (6:3).

Several years ago, I happened to drive by Forest Lawn Cemetery in Los Angeles. Two delightful elderly women were my passengers. One was in her nineties, and the other was nearly that age. Just as we passed Forest Lawn, an airplane flew over us on its way to the Burbank airport. One of the women peered at the cemetery through the smog and in a serious voice declared, "I wouldn't want to be buried there. Too noisy."

We joke about burial, but it was no joking matter in ancient Israel. Repeatedly, the Old Testament refers to the ignominy of death without burial. For instance, when Jeremiah the prophet uttered the judgment of the Lord against Jehoiakim, the king of Judah, the greatest insult he hurled against him touched on this issue: "They will not mourn for him: 'Alas, my brother! Alas, my sister!' They will not mourn for him: 'Alas, my master! Alas, his splendor!' He will have the burial of a donkey—dragged away and thrown outside the gates of Jerusalem" (Jer. 22:18,19).

Isaiah also refers to the horrible circumstances of not having one's body rest in the grave (see Isa. 14:18,19). In both cases, the horror of being unburied or having one's grave vandalized is a matter of the greatest concern. To suffer either would be a disgrace.

Solomon says, "Look at that man. He has all this wealth and all those children, and yet he is unhappy; and his children don't care enough about him to give him a decent burial. A stillborn child is better off than he is." (Job 3:16 and Psalm 58:8 also refer to instances where someone would have been better off to have been stillborn; this is a figurative way to express evil experienced at its worst.)

In verses 4-6 of Ecclesiastes 6 Solomon reminds us that all of us die, rich and poor alike. His point is that since we all live only once and then die, it would be tragic to fail to enjoy our lives, regardless of the reason. What good is wealth if we are not able to enjoy ourselves while we have it? And since we cannot know in advance whether or not we will enjoy wealth once it is ours, why pursue it? Since we only go around once in life, why not accept the providence of God and make the most of what He will give us if we will accept it!

Who Knows Whether Wealth Will Satisfy?

Solomon touches on a sore nerve when he moves to this question. Since chapter 5, verse 10, he has been discussing it in one way or another. He becomes quite pointed here.

At first glance it seems as if his comments are exaggerated.

"All man's efforts are for his mouth, yet his appetite is never satisfied" (Eccles. 6:7).

He made a similar observation in the book of Proverbs: "The laborer's appetite works for him; his hunger drives him on" (Prov. 16:26). What is he saying? Does he mean these words literally? Or is he intending to speak in broader terms? While the immediate reference is to food, I believe his intention is to speak of anything material. No matter what they are, material things do not satisfy our souls. There is a sense in which our lives are filled with working so we can eat, and eating so we can find the strength to keep on working. On and on it goes. It is an endless cycle, a vanity.

Obviously, we do not take this sort of verdict without a fight. Solomon knows his secular opponent is not going to like it either, so he follows his assertion about food with another bold claim.

> What advantage has a wise man over a fool? What
> does a poor man gain by knowing how to conduct him-
> self before others? (Eccles. 6:8).

It may be better to have wisdom than folly (see 2:13), but our experience shows us that a wise person does not necessarily have more than a fool. "A fool and his money are soon parted," the old saying goes; but the fact that he had it to lose in the first place proves that even fools do quite well for themselves occasionally! We already have discovered that the wise person's wisdom brings him sorrow (see 2:15,16); he sees the truth about life's vanity clearly, while the fool wallows in his ignorant folly.

The second half of Ecclesiastes 6:8 asks what the poor get for walking an upright life. The answer is the same as for the wise: nobody really knows. They may be better off, or they may not be. How are we to know for sure? In either case, both questions point to the next verse.

> Better what the eye sees than the roving of the appe-
> tite. This too is meaningless, a chasing after the wind
> (6:9).

Another way of saying this is, "It is better to be content with what you see (see 11:9) than to let your desires wander to what others have (see 4:4). To strive after these things is like chasing the wind." Better to enjoy what we have than to be filled with restlessness or envy over what is not ours. Matthew 6:33 says, "But seek first his kingdom and his righteousness." When our first desire is God's kingdom, then He can trust us with our desires.

We should not work for the purpose of material gain. Of course we must work, but we should do so for the glory of God. We need to be content with what God gives us. "All man's efforts are for his mouth," says Solomon, "yet his appetite is never satisfied" (Eccles. 6:7). We have no way of knowing whether our financial goals will bring us satisfaction if we meet them.

Who Knows Whether Wealth Will Be Good For Us?

Solomon concludes his argument in this section of Ecclesiastes with some interesting questions; few people on the road to wealth ever bother to ask them. "When I get it, how do I know it will be good for me? Will it be worth the cost? Maybe down the road I will need patience, and all I will have is a pile of gold at several hundred dollars per ounce. Maybe I will need strength of character, and all I will have is a fortune. Maybe I will need hope instead of money."

> Whatever exists has already been named, and what
> man is has been known; no man can contend with one
> who is stronger than he. The more the words, the less
> the meaning, and how does that profit anyone? For
> who knows what is good for a man in life, during the
> few and meaningless days he passes through like a
> shadow? Who can tell him what will happen under the
> sun after he is gone? (6:10-12).

God already has a plan; He also knows that we are merely human, nothing more. It is interesting to note that at both 1:9

and 3:15 the same point is made. We cannot alter who we are, and we cannot alter the world God has made. We came from the dust, and we will return to the dust (see Gen. 2:19; 3:19). We are human beings. That is the all-important reality. God has made us in His image, but we still are mortal creatures. Only He is immortal.

"What man is has been known; no man can contend with one who is stronger than he" (Eccles. 6:10). It is futile to fight with God; He always wins.

When Solomon says that we cannot fight with God, he is warning us not to strive for our own plans. Instead, we should fit into God's plans. Since His plan is perfect in every way, it would be foolish (vain) indeed for us to want to go our own way. His way has to be better than ours.

The key to this whole section lies in the next verse, "For who knows what is good for a man in life, during the few and meaningless days he passes through like a shadow?" (6:12). "Our lives pass so quickly," he says. This image is reminiscent of Psalm 102:11, where the psalmist complains that his days are not only like a shadow, but they are like a shadow that lengthens—a short day at that! Solomon concludes, "Who can tell him what will happen under the sun after he is gone?"

Solomon is not talking about heaven or hell in these verses; he is talking about life "under the sun"—life here and now. We do not know what the future "under the sun" will bring; and since we do not know what is in the future, how do we know whether wealth would be to our advantage?

It is a fair question. At the end of Ecclesiastes Solomon will tell us that the key to everything lies in two truths: "Fear God and keep his commandments" (12:13). For now, though, he is content to raise the question nobody can answer.

We simply do not know what we need. We do not know it now; we will not know it in the future either.

Once again, Solomon's insights have different meanings for those who believe than they do for secularists. These bold statements remind the believer that the present and the future are in good hands. Those who cannot allow room for a loving Father God in this world are caught on the horns of a dilemma. They see the truth of what Solomon says: they have no way of knowing whether they will enjoy the wealth they crave. And they have no way of knowing whether it will be good for them or bad. Until they are ready to trust Solomon's God, they are stuck on those horns.

For the one who believes, there is no such dilemma; there are no horns on which we may be impaled. Instead, there are arms, arms of the loving Father whose every desire is for the best for all His children.

No good thing does he withhold from those whose
walk is blameless (Ps. 84:11).

Questions for Discussion

1. Have you, like Solomon, questioned the true value of wealth? What value do you place on material and financial security? Is your view of the value of wealth out of proportion?
2. Have you found that, like John Rockefeller, your desire for riches has increased as your financial situation has improved? If so, how does this make you feel?
3. Someone once said, "We spend money we don't have on things we don't need to impress people we don't like." Do you feel this statement applies to you? Why? Why not?
4. As you see your life today, would more wealth be beneficial or detrimental to your walk with the Lord? Why would there be a change?
5. Someone else has said, "We should swing free from all that is not eternal." Do you agree? To what extent is your view of material things an eternal one? What are some steps toward doing this?

CHAPTER SEVEN

Wisdom and Suffering

Ecclesiastes 7:1-29

I believe W. C. Fields is the one credited with the remark, "I've been rich and I've been poor. I'd rather be rich." If we were to apply his statement to suffering, we might say, "I've had trouble and I've not had it. I'd rather not have it." We would wonder about the emotional health of someone who preferred suffering and misery to health and happiness.

But is "Thanks, but no thanks!" the only thing we can say about suffering?"

I think of Karl Kassulke who played strong safety for the Minnesota Vikings for 10 seasons. Karl was known for his reckless life-style, both on and off the football field. Then a freak motorcycle accident on a suburban interstate highway ended his career, and he was left with a severed spine and paralysis in most of his body. Suffering? Yes. Tragedy? His own verdict: "Obviously, I didn't think I needed that motorcycle accident. But that was what it took to bring me to my knees. I don't think I ever would have done it otherwise. It was what I needed. It was God's grace to me."[1]

So suffering is not *always* evil! It is not always "meaningless." Value can come from it, too.

Jesus understood suffering. He knew its value, and He knew

He would suffer. "The Son of Man must suffer many things" (Luke 9:22) was how He faced the suffering He would endure. If He had been unwilling to suffer on our behalf, how different the world would be. None of us would be saved; we would not be reconciled to God. So there was great value in the suffering of Jesus.

Could there be great value in our suffering? Scripture makes it clear: we are called by God to suffer. "For it has been granted to you on behalf of Christ not only to believe in him, but also to suffer for him" (Phil. 1:29). "But rejoice that you participate in the sufferings of Christ . . . . If you suffer as a Christian, do not be ashamed, but praise God that you bear that name" (1 Pet. 4:13,16). There is more to suffering than meets the eye.

Solomon has a way of turning the tables on us. While we desire wealth and dislike suffering, he sees them both differently. In Ecclesiastes 6 he declares that the value of riches is uncertain and prosperity is not necessarily good. Then in chapter 7 he says that adversity, or suffering, is not necessarily evil.

Some plants thrive better in darkness than in light; some qualities grow better in adversity than in ease. This is not always true; some plants wither and die in the darkness, and some people are destroyed by suffering. There is one thing of which we can be sure, though. Sooner or later, suffering will come our way. The question is, will we benefit from it? Or will it destroy us?

In this section of Ecclesiastes Solomon continues his confrontation with the secular mindset. He says, "Let's take a close look at suffering and affliction. Sooner or later, you or someone you love will face suffering. What will it mean? How will you handle it?" Of course, once again it will have very different meanings for those who love and serve the Lord than it will for those who do not.

How does God use adversity for good?

Better than Laughter

Better is an important word in Ecclesiastes. It is used 23 times throughout the book, but nowhere more regularly than here (four times in four verses), and certainly nowhere in a more striking way. It is as if Solomon says, "Let your sorrow make you better, not bitter."

A good name is better than fine perfume, and the day of death better than the day of birth. It is better to go to a house of mourning than to go to a house of feasting, for death is the destiny of every man; the living should take this to heart. Sorrow is better than laughter, because a sad face is good for the heart. The heart of the wise is in the house of mourning, but the heart of fools is in the house of pleasure (Eccles. 7:1-4).

In Proverbs 17:22 Solomon wrote, "A cheerful heart is good medicine, but a crushed spirit dries up the bones." So he is not speaking against laughter or happiness as a matter of principle. He must have had another point in mind.

If Solomon intended to shock his audience with Ecclesiastes 7:1, he certainly must have been pleased with its results. The assertion that the day of one's death is better than the day of one's birth comes at us with no warning. Certainly, he was not referring to life after death, as the apostle Paul was when he wrote, "I desire to depart and be with Christ, which is better" (Phil. 1:23). The subject here is life, here and now.

Solomon is comparing two days—the day of birth and the day of death. His comparison, "A good name is better than fine perfume" is parallel to "the day of death [is] better than the day of birth" (Eccles. 7:1). Precious ointment was a perfume used on happy occasions, as on the day of a birth. It was precious, but not as precious as a good name. You can buy the ointment; a good name cannot be purchased for any price. So some things are definitely better than others. But how can the day of death be better than the day of life?

The answer is in verse 2: "It is better to go to a house of mourning than to go to a house of feasting, for death is the destiny of every man; the living should take this to heart." We learn more through death than through birth. None of us learned much at our birth. We do not learn much at the birth of someone else, either. It is a day of rejoicing. It is a happy time, but we learn very little of ultimate value. There is so much, though, to learn at the time of death!

The psalmist wrote, "Teach us to number our days aright, that we may gain a heart of wisdom" (Ps. 90:12). The day of death is a day when we number our days. We look at our lives and take stock; we become fertile soil for the growth of God's Word. Eventually our own death will come.

Solomon also said that sorrow has a refining influence on us (see Eccles. 7:3,4). He does not say that we should have sorrow instead of laughter; sorrow is merely "better." There is a value system at work here—good, better, and best. Through sorrow our hearts are made better.

Again, Solomon's words will have different meanings to the believer and the unbeliever. To the unbeliever, the only reason to take note of death is to be sure not to let any of life's gusto slip through one's fingers. Solomon acknowledges this in verse 4: "The heart of fools is in the house of pleasure." The fool wants to repress all thought of the inevitability of death.

The Christian, though, sees a very different message in Solomon's wisdom. In tough times our hearts are softened and made pliable in God's hands. "No discipline seems pleasant at the time, but painful. Later on, however, it produces a harvest of righteousness and peace for those who have been trained by it" (Heb. 12:11).

"When all kinds of trials and temptations crowd into your lives, my brothers, don't resent them as intruders, but welcome them as friends! Realize that they come to test your faith and to produce in you the quality of endurance. But let the process go on until that endurance is fully developed, and you will find you have become men of mature character, men of integrity, with no weak spots" (James 1:2-4, *Phillips*).

God does not waste sorrow or adversity. He knows the purpose for which we go through tragedy and sorrow. It is for our good, and the good of His kingdom.

Better Than Praise

Certainly, it is easier to receive praise than rebuke, praise is also easier to give. The wise person will carefully listen to the rebukes he receives. Frequently they contain a great deal more love than praise does: "It is better to heed a wise man's rebuke than to listen to the song of fools" (Eccles. 7:5). It is better to be rebuked by a wise person than to be complimented by a fool.

In another place Solomon wrote, "The kisses of an enemy may be profuse, but faithful are the wounds of a friend" (Prov. 27:6). I have learned some of the most important lessons of my life when a friend cared enough for me to risk our friendship and tell me what I needed to know. I do not recall ever liking to hear it, even if I smiled while the words were being said. Not once! But when I have been willing to swallow my pride and get on my knees before God, I've learned my most important lessons. "Faithful are the wounds of a friend." Indeed!

If we are unwilling to be rebuked or corrected, we will go through life unaware of much of what God wants for us. Husbands, wives, and children ought to think about this. Who on the face of all the earth loves us more than our spouses or our parents? Whose advice should we be able to trust more?

The Laughter of the Fool

There is humor in Ecclesiastes 7:6: "Like the crackling of thorns under the pot, so is the laughter of fools. This too is meaningless."

Whenever I light my fireplace on a cool winter evening, I have a choice. I can either hold my match under a pile of kindling or under a large log. If I go the kindling route, the match will quickly cause a fire. If I try to light the log, nothing happens. However, if I have a fire made of logs, it will burn for hours; but if I am content to use twigs and kindling only, my fire will either flame fast and burn out quickly or I will have to continue feeding it every few minutes.

So it is with a fire made of crackling thorns. There is little to it. Oh, it is a noisy fire, much like the laughter of the fool is filled with much noise. The irony is that at first it appears as if it is a better fire than the one made correctly. There is much noise and light, and it spreads its warmth quickly. But its heat is negligible because it comes and goes in a few seconds. So is the praise of fools. It is "vain," empty and without substance.

Better Than Fretting

I was preparing to preach on the subject, "Love is patient" from 1 Corinthians 13:4. I decided to take a break and pick up a new part for my son's stereo. As I was driving to the store, the man following me crashed into the rear of my nearly new car! After I called the police to report the accident, it seemed (to this preacher who was in the midst of preparing a sermon on patience!) as if they took forever to arrive. Once I was finished with them, I decided to get an estimate for the repair to my car and called ahead so I would not have to wait long. Anyone who ever has been in a rush knows the rest of the story! Delay followed delay. Finally, the Lord had to remind me of my sermon: Love is patient. It is patient not just with those we know well, but also with strangers.

> Extortion turns a wise man into a fool, and a bribe corrupts the heart. The end of a matter is better than its beginning, and patience is better than pride. Do not be quickly provoked in your spirit, for anger resides in the lap of fools. Do not say, "Why were the old days better than these?" For it is not wise to ask such questions (Eccles. 7:8-10).

There is much wisdom in these verses. The problems Solomon discusses in them—worry, impatience, pride, anger, romanticizing the past—seem to plague each generation. Why does he talk about them here? And why does he bring them together the way he does?

Remember that Solomon is talking about what is better. Now Solomon moves on to these immature ways in which we indulge ourselves and which only serve to defeat us.

When he says, "The end of a matter is better than its beginning" Solomon is warning us to look at the big picture, not the smallness of beginnings or the setbacks we incur. We should be patient; we should not be deterred or discouraged along the way. If God is in something, then we know it will be successful according to His purpose for it. We can rest in that.

Furthermore, patience is important. "And patience is better than pride" (v. 8). Patience and pride are opposites; a proud person is seldom a patient one. The proud person is self-centered; he is not patient with others. "Love is patient" (1 Cor. 13:4). When we truly love others, we will be patient with them. But if our primary interest is in getting what *we* want from life, we will be impatient. So self-centeredness and impatience go together, as do humility and patience.

How does the fool handle the frustrations of life? Solomon tells us: "Do not be quickly provoked in your spirit, for anger resides in the lap of fools" (Eccles. 7:9). The fool's approach to his problems is anger. Even on a merely pragmatic, secular basis the fool's response makes no sense! When he is angry, he loses his ability to think clearly and gets himself in even worse trouble.

This is a place where we believers must apply our theology. We know that God is going to accomplish His purposes on earth. We know the results of history in advance—God wins! So if I am a child of His, I can say: "I know I am His child and will share in His victory. Therefore, rather than being impatient or angry with life, I can look forward in faith to the day when God will bring in His kingdom."

Solomon cuts through the futility of worrying with the words, "Do not say, 'Why were the old days better than these?'" (7:10). Nowhere does the folly of our impatience show through better than here. The person who laments the passing of the "good old days" does not remember them very well. I would not trade today for those days for anything. These are the days God has given me! And furthermore, I like life today.

People long for the past for several reasons. The first is a poor memory (perhaps it would be better to call it a creative memory!). The second is that it is easier to escape from today's realities through nostalgia than it is to handle today's problems.

Third, it is easier to complain than to deal with problems constructively. If we take responsibility for today, we are making a commitment to work for a better world. Fourth, it is often a childish, immature way of expressing disappointment. It is much like the child who decides to take his ball and go home when the game does not go his way.

Solomon knew all this; and he declares, "For it is not wise to ask such questions" (7:10). We are fools when we long for a previous "golden age," as foolish as Ponce de León was when he sought the fountain of youth. One era is basically like all others (see 1:9,10).

It is easy for Christians today to be discouraged. Immorality is flaunted on every side. An abortion is as easy to get as a new set of tires. Business leaders corrupt politicians, and corrupted politicians seek even larger bribes. In far too many homes family life has degenerated into a quarrelsome battleground.

Yet, in the face of these discouraging realities, we need to remember the One who will have the last word. One day the blast of God's trumpet will ring forth from heaven, and God's new age will begin.

Whatever our fears, or whatever uncertainties we must learn to accept, we must not cry, "Why were the old days better than these?" They never were. But even more important, the end—the completion—of God's work is even better than its beginning.

The Excellence of Wisdom

We are constantly making decisions. Sometimes we make right ones, and other times we make wrong ones. The person who wants to serve the Lord desires to know God's will and obey Him more than anything else, but many other factors get in the way. We are bombarded with all sorts of temptations to compromise or confuse us—greed, lust, envy, fear, pride, self-love. Our culture preaches consumerism and hedonism, both boldly and subtly. If ever God's people needed wisdom for the living of their lives, it is today. There are far too many distractions that would blur our vision.

In another book Solomon declared, "The beginning of wisdom is this: Get wisdom, and whatever you get, get insight" (Prov. 4:7, *RSV*). In another chapter of that book he wrote, "The fear of the Lord is the beginning of knowledge (1:7). In other words, if you want to get wisdom, get on with it! Begin by fearing God.

What does it mean to fear God? Certainly it includes an element of being afraid of God; after all, He is the Almighty! But the fear of the Lord includes much more; it includes one's whole relationship with God. We are to reverence Him, to honor Him, to worship and adore Him—with all that we are. That is what it means to fear the Lord. We may have knowledge about Him without reverencing or honoring or worshiping Him. We will not see life as God sees it, and we will not know what He expects of us. We will not have wisdom.

Wisdom Is a Protection

When I look back on the mistakes I have made and the sins I have committed, I am amazed that they always have come from not living within the wisdom of God. Solomon experienced that, too. He knew there was a protection in God's wisdom, and he knew we can only enjoy that protection when we obey God.

> Wisdom, like an inheritance, is a good thing and benefits those who see the sun. Wisdom is a shelter as money is a shelter, but the advantage of knowledge is this: that wisdom preserves the life of its possessor. Consider what God has done: Who can straighten what he has made crooked? When times are good, be happy; but when times are bad, consider: God has made the one as well as the other. Therefore, a man cannot discover anything about his future (Eccles. 7:11-14).

Solomon seems to be thinking of wisdom in terms of the gain it brings us. This is quite unlike his comments in Proverbs where he declares wisdom to be priceless: "For wisdom is more precious than rubies, and nothing you desire can compare with her" (8:11). In practical terms, even if we were to inherit vast wealth, we would still need wisdom to protect us from our foolishness (see Eccles. 7:11). Furthermore, wisdom will be "profitable" only to the living, "to those who see the sun" (7:11). We must obtain its benefits now; wisdom will do us no good once we are dead.

In light of this it is refreshing to note Solomon's comments concerning wisdom: "She is a tree of life to those who embrace her" (Prov. 3:18). "For whoever finds [wisdom] finds life and receives favor from the Lord" (Prov. 8:35). Wisdom is life-giving in the sense that whoever finds it is in touch with the life of God.

It is important to remember the historical situation when Solomon penned these words. Israel was experiencing success and wealth unlike anything it had ever known, but it had begun to deteriorate from within, first in its leadership and then throughout the nation. Because of its wealth, Israel was able to buy some protection through alliances. The people understood the power that wealth brings; Solomon knew it was also important for them to realize that wisdom is superior to wealth. Its "advantage" is that it "preserves the life of its possessor" (Eccles. 7:12). This is true on a national level when nations try to use their wealth and power to control events to their advantage and on the personal level when individuals seek to "buy" the esteem of others. It is "better" to follow the Lord and seek His wisdom. The protection that wealth purchases is always for sale to the highest bidder.

Earlier in Ecclesiastes Solomon has written, "What is twisted cannot be straightened; what is lacking cannot be counted" (1:15). That is, it does no good to wish we could change those things over which we have no control.

Ecclesiastes 7:13 reminds us once again of the crooked things. They are crooked from our vantage point; we see them as being to our disadvantage. For the one who leaves God out of the picture, this verdict is a discouragement; for the believer, however, it is a reminder of God's sovereignty. God loves the world; He loves us; His activities are always good.

All of us have "crooked" places—physical appearance, relatives, job, economic situations, health—whatever. A believer can accept them, knowing that the sovereign God knows best. This is not a call to stoic passivity, as if we are to accept everything about life without thinking. But there are "crooked" things we cannot straighten, and we must learn to believe and say: "God, you are God. You are good and powerful. I trust you. I believe in you. And even though I don't like some of these things that come from your hand, by faith I accept them with joy."

The only thing that can keep us from affirming these "crooked" things as blessings from the Lord is a temporal, secular value system. It says: "I am only concerned about right now; the future isn't important. I'm more concerned about my comfort and convenience than I am about godliness and being available to the Lord." A secular value system has no room for a sovereign God (other than self). Consequently, when we realize that the earth is God's and He is its Lord, the secular viewpoint is seen for the foolishness it is. It offers no gain.

We are to be joyful in good times as in bad (see v. 14). God made both of them. Our inclination is to accept "prosperity" and reject "adversity." If we *knew* what the future was going to bring, we would be even more inclined to do whatever comes to mind. "After all," we might say, "if this is what will happen for sure, it makes no difference what I do." However, if we are dependent on God at each step of the way, we must pay attention as each step is taken.

We must allow God to be large enough that we can trust Him in the day of prosperity and not let that prosperity turn us from the course. It is equally important that we let Him be large enough that our faith is not damaged or destroyed in the day of adversity. God has His purposes for both.

The wisdom of God protects us. If we live in it, we trust Him in both straight and crooked places, joy and sorrow, success or failure. Wisdom says, "Trust Him. He knows more than you do. He cares about you." "He who did not spare his own Son, but gave him up for us all—how will he not also, along with him, graciously give us all things?" (Rom. 8:32).

What protection there is in that!

Wisdom Is a Strength

Wisdom is more than protection; it is also strength.

> In this meaningless life of mine I have seen both of
> these: a righteous man perishing in his righteousness,
> and a wicked man living long in his wickedness. Do not
> be overrighteous, neither be overwise—why destroy
> yourself? Do not be overwicked, and do not be a
> fool—why die before your time? It is good to grasp
> the one and not let go of the other. The man who fears
> God will avoid all extremes. Wisdom makes one wise
> man more powerful than ten rulers in a city (Eccles.
> 7:15-19).

Once again Solomon picks up on the secularist's attitude toward wisdom. "What good is it?" he might ask. "When good men die and wicked men prosper, what is the point of living by wisdom?" From his point of view, the secularist makes sense. If faith is unknown or ignored, there seems to be no purpose in wisdom.

Furthermore, the advice not to be overly righteous, wise, or wicked sounds very sensible to the secularist. The Chinese are reported to have a saying, "The shoot that grows tall is the first to be cut." It expresses much the same thought as we find in verses 15 through 18. Solomon's point in including these words is to show that this is the logical conclusion of a secular person's life.

But the secularist's mind-set is not the only thing at work in these verses. "Wisdom makes one wise man more powerful than ten rulers in a city" (7:19). I believe that Solomon is saying: "Yes, you are right—from your limited vantage point. If you rule out a loving, sovereign God to begin with, it does make a lot of sense to avoid being too good or too evil. You will want to keep your options open. However, if all this talk about God *is* true, then wisdom will strengthen you more than many wise rulers will strengthen a city."

A Christian will see through this argument quite quickly.

Obviously, Solomon does not mean the words *righteous* or *wicked* in their absolute senses. Only God is absolutely holy or righteous; it is ludicrous to talk of a "righteous" person, just as it is absurd to talk of a "wicked" person, as if we were not all sinners. (Of course, the Christian knows that everyone who is in Christ is made righteous and holy [see Rom. 3:22,26; 4:11].)

But the person who follows in God's way experiences a different reality. His wisdom brings success. His path gets there! God's ways protect him from errors and excesses. The One who made us knows what is best for us. That is why we must seek the wisdom that only comes from God. It is our strength in the midst of a world that has lost its reason for living.

Wisdom Is Scarce

Having declared the protection and strength of wisdom, Solomon looks around himself and says, "There aren't many wise people." He begins with the cause of this condition: "There is not a righteous man on earth who does what is right and never sins" (Eccles. 7:20).

"There is not a righteous man on earth" reminds us of Romans, chapter 3: "There is not one righteous, not even one; there is no one who understands, no one who seeks God. All have turned away, they have together become worthless; there is no one who does good, not even one" (Rom. 3:10-12).

When Solomon says, "there is not a righteous man on earth," he is stating a fact, not offering an excuse. Indeed, he is declaring his own faith.

In the previous section he argued the case of the secularist to show that wisdom provides more strength than human knowledge. The way of the secularist leads to defeat and weakness; the way of wisdom leads to victory and strength. Here, however, he argues from the position of faith in God and reminds us of a basic Scripture truth: the problem with humanity is sin. This is the basis for every word he utters; it is the reason so few people are wise. They are bound up in their unrighteousness, their sin.

This sin problem expresses itself in our relationship with others (see Rom. 1–3 for a full analysis of this problem). Later in Ecclesiastes 7, Solomon will deal with the alienation between the sexes, but first he uses an illustration from work, the master and the servant. We might speak of it as the employer and the employee.

> Do not pay attention to every word people say, or you may hear your servant cursing you—for you know in your heart that many times you yourself have cursed others (7:21,22).

Here Solomon is referring to destructive, not constructive, criticism. And who of us has not been stung by adverse criticism? Solomon says we ought to take it with a grain of salt. If there is something to be learned from criticism, then be thankful for it. But if we hear censure that is unfair, we should not become upset. After all, what difference does it make if it is unfair? We have been unkind and unfair toward others ourselves! Solomon gives us a dismal verdict:

> All this I tested by wisdom and I said, "I am determined to be wise"—but this was beyond me. Whatever wisdom may be, it is far off and most profound—who can discover it? (7:23,24).

There is a sense, of course, in which those who have walked with God a long time have gained much wisdom; but that does not seem to be what Solomon is driving at here. Rather, he seems to be saying that after his elaborate search for wisdom he failed to find it. He could even be expressing the thoughts a secular person might have after carefully thinking through each of the areas Solomon has explored.

His verdict—"This was beyond me . . . who can discover it?"—is the cry of every person who has sought the meaning of life apart from God. It cannot be found there.

So he turns to relationships; but they, like everything else, are marred by sin.

So I turned my mind to understand, to investigate and
to search out wisdom and the scheme of things and to
understand the stupidity of wickedness and the madness of folly. I find more bitter than death the woman
who is a snare, whose heart is a trap and whose hands
are chains. The man who pleases God will escape her,
but the sinner she will ensnare. "Look," says the
Teacher, "this is what I have discovered: Adding one
thing to another to discover the scheme of things—
while I was still searching but not finding—I found one
upright man among a thousand, but not one upright,
woman among them all" (7:25-28).

When Solomon speaks of "the wickedness of folly," he is saying that nothing is more stupid than folly, or sin. He applies his
lesson to the adulterous woman, a subject of which it seems rea-
sonable to assume Solomon had intimate knowledge (in view of
his thousand wives and concubines, see 1 Kings 11:3). The sin
he describes in Ecclesiastes 7:26 cheapens and distorts even
the closest and most intimate relationship with which God
blessed humanity (see Gen. 2:24).

There is no point in documenting the rampant immorality of
our time; it is all too apparent. It is also apparent, however, that
even Christians find themselves wondering if perhaps the biblical
commands against fornication and adultery are outmoded. Solomon's own life was certainly a disaster at this point. However,
his experience also gave him ample reason to reflect on the
meaning of his sin, and God used him to pen some of the Scripture's most vivid warnings about the dangers of fornication and
adultery.

In Proverbs Solomon wrote that if you follow wisdom, you
will be saved from immorality.

For wisdom will enter your heart, and knowledge will
be pleasant to your soul. Discretion will protect you,
and understanding will guard you. It will save you also
from the adulteress, from the wayward wife with her
seductive words, who has left the partner of her youth

and ignored the covenant she made before God. For her house leads down to death and her paths to the spirits of the dead. None who go to her return or attain the paths of life (Prov. 2:10,11,16-19).

Is immorality serious or not? "None who go to her return or attain the paths of life." It is not that God will not forgive sexual sin; He does and will. But this sin marks us in a way no other sin does, and we never quite get over it. The longer I have pastored and the more people with whom I have counseled, the more I see the truth of Solomon's verdict worked out in human experience.

Wisdom will keep us from immorality. If we fail, God's forgiveness will cleanse us from the guilt of sin once we confess it and repent. Solomon speaks so strongly against this sin because he knew its devastating impact personally. We should not take his words lightly.

I have yet to find a commentator who offers a completely satisfactory explanation as to why Solomon said that he was able to find one righteous man among a thousand, but not one woman. Surely he was aware of the stories of the godly judge Deborah (see Judg. 4:5) and of Samuel's godly mother Hannah (see 1 Sam. 1–2). It seems too simple to merely pass him off as a male chauvinist; for in Proverbs 12:4; 14:1; 18:22; 19:14; and 31:10-31 he speaks very highly of women.

Perhaps the clue to this question is to be found by regarding the phrase "one righteous man among a thousand" as a Hebrew equivalent to our "one in a million." If this is the case, his comment about women could be an equally idiomatic way of speaking of women. Frankly, there is not much difference between one in a thousand and none!

Regardless, it is obvious what the punch line of Solomon's comment is in verse 29: "This only have I found: God made mankind upright, but men have gone in search of many schemes" (Eccles. 7:29).

Granted, wisdom is rare in a man (or in a woman). Why? Men and women are sinners (see 7:20) and have "gone in search of many schemes" even though God made them upright. Later,

Isaiah would pen the same sentiments in another period of Israel's history: "We all, like sheep, have gone astray, each of us has turned to his own way" (Isa. 53:6). Isaiah went on to speak of the grace of God in the second half of the verse: "And the Lord has laid on him [Jesus] the iniquity of us all."

Solomon does not talk of a Deliverer in these verses, but his picture of humanity certainly demands one. Instead, he points us to the beginning: "God made man upright" (Eccles. 7:29). Once we know that, we can see that our folly is our own doing. But by telling us that God made us upright—morally straight—in the beginning, Solomon reminds us that there is more to life than the vanities the book of Ecclesiastes so eloquently proclaims.

NOTE
1. Karl Kassulke and Ron Pitkin, *Kassulke* (Nashville, TN: Thomas Nelson Publishers, 1981), p. 219.

Questions for Discussion

1. The author proclaims that "suffering is not *always* evil." How has your life proven this statement to be true?
2. Is your faith such that you can believe that God can make both the bad and good times beneficial?
3. What kinds of suffering do you face because of your relationship with Christ? How have such incidents helped you to identify with the suffering that Christ endured?
4. Have you ever faced death? What have you learned during these times?
5. When in your life have the "wounds of a friend" proved to be faithful and beneficial?
6. Which seems better to you—the good ol' days, or the days that are to come? Have you acknowledged that God holds both in His hands?

7. In Ecclesiastes 2:12-16, Solomon declares that wisdom is meaningless, because both the wise and the foolish must die. Yet, in Ecclesiastes 7:11,12, Solomon describes wisdom as an inheritance and a shelter. How do you explain this apparent discrepancy?

CHAPTER EIGHT

When Our Vision Isn't 20/20

Ecclesiastes 8:1-17

I know of no one who better illustrates humanity's distorted vision than the cartoon character of television fame, Mr. Magoo. Magoo has the uncanny misfortune of completely misinterpreting every situation he encounters. His circumstances are frequently ludicrous, and sometimes potentially disastrous; but somehow Mr. Magoo keeps on muddling and stumbling through life, much like the kitten whose eyes have not yet opened to the world.

I find it easy to identify with Mr. Magoo; sometimes my vision is blinded by circumstances. But Mr. Magoo has a broader symbolic meaning than any one person's experiences; he is a parable of humanity. Granted, few people ever encounter the comic situations in which he frequently is placed, but all of us do have great difficult "seeing" things as they really are. Our vision is limited. We can only see for short distances, and we are limited by time.

Throughout Ecclesiastes, Solomon has repeatedly asked us to look at life very carefully, to see it for what it is. As a result, we have explored many areas with him—wisdom, pleasure, fulfillment, good, evil, work, friendship, wealth. In the process we have discovered that everything about life has a different meaning for those who have faith in God than it does for those who live a secular life-style.

If we take the secularist at his word and look at the world only in terms of what we can see, touch, taste, and smell (empiricism), we will be led to despair. We cannot count on the things we love or possess; they can be taken away from us. And even if no one ever takes them from us, ultimately death will take us from them. Since that is the sum total of life "under the sun," it is a pretty devastating verdict for the secularist to face.

Life looks very different to believers. Since we know that life continues into eternity, we are not threatened by death. Rather, death is seen as merely one experience in life among many. And since the believer trusts in an infinite, personal, and loving God, death can take away nothing important. This God we love loves us unconditionally, and He can be trusted.

At this point in his argument, Solomon takes a slightly modified course; he reminds those of us who love and serve the Lord that our vision is not 20/20 either. There are realities of life that defy our understanding, no matter how intelligent we are or how sincere our faith is.

The truth, of course, is that our vision never has been 20/20. Verse 29 of chapter 7 has reminded us of that already: "This only I have found: God made mankind upright, but men have gone in search of many schemes." Our "schemes" have distorted our vision, and Solomon asks us to consider what our limited vision means when we face the uncomfortable, inscrutable realities of life.

When Our Leaders Abuse Us

It is significant that when Solomon begins to discuss our relationship to rulers, he begins with a word of caution. Whether we face the capricious tyranny that frequently exists under a king (as was the case in the biblical world) or a dictator (which is more common in our own time) or whether we must deal with the powerful vested interests in our own democratic society, it is wise to be discreet when dealing with anyone who has real authority over us. Listen to Solomon's advice in Ecclesiastes 8:1-4:

Who is like the wise man? Who knows the explanation
of things? Wisdom brightens a man's face and changes
its hard appearance. Obey the king's command, I say,
because you took an oath before God. Do not be in a
hurry to leave the king's presence. Do not stand up
for a bad cause, for he will do whatever he pleases.
Since a king's word is supreme, who can say to him,
"What are you doing?"

Who of us really knows enough to know *exactly* what God is
doing in our time? And who of us knows enough to know what
our own rulers are planning? No one.

We have our opinions, and we probably would prefer to hear
some things, rather than others, from our leaders. However,
none of us knows what is in the hearts of men and women—
much less God's heart—and none of us knows what the future
will bring.

Solomon speaks of the wise man's face being bright—or
shining. There is something to be learned from this expression.
Solomon is not telling us to be wise and fake it; he is saying that
we should be joyful, no matter what the circumstances are. We
are to be a blessing, not a curse. Repeatedly, the writers of
Scripture use the image of a shining face to speak of blessing. In
the book of Numbers we read, "The Lord bless you and keep
you, the Lord make his face shine upon you and be gracious to
you" (6:24,25). The Psalms repeatedly refer to the Lord's face
"shining" upon His people (see Ps. 31:16; 67:1; 80:3,7,19;
119:135).

Also, they speak of God's being the source of our blessing:
"Those who look to him are radiant" (Ps. 34:5). When His face
shines on us, we are blessed. When our faces shine on the
world, we bless it. That is how we are to *begin* to deal with those
in authority over us. We are to be a blessing unto them, even
when they are insensitive or cruel.

We are not asked to give up our beliefs, though. We are
asked to deal with adversity in the same spirit as Jesus did when
He prayed from the cross, "Father, forgive them" (Luke 23:34).
When peace and joy and praise rule in our hearts, they will show

through in every circumstance, not just in those we select for ourselves.

A wise person will realize that more is going on in this world than meets the eye. God is in control. He will raise up leaders and rulers, and He will cast down those who oppress His people—in His own good time (see Ps. 2). Rather than walk around with a stern, sad, "cursing" face, it is better to bless those who have authority over us.

Solomon's words at this point are very practical. We instinctively know he is right when he cautions us to obey the king or the ruler. Who has the power to question his actions and get away with it? Instead we are to be discreet and know that those in authority—be they our boss, the government, or whatever—have the power to enforce their demands, whether we like it or not.

This is not the whole picture; it is only the beginning. There is an accounting to be made for the way power is used, and Solomon speaks about it quite forthrightly.

> Whoever obeys his command will come to no harm,
> and the wise heart will know the proper time and pro-
> cedure. For there is a proper time and procedure for
> every matter, though a man's misery weighs heavily
> upon him. Since no man knows the future, who can tell
> him what is to come? No man has power over the
> wind to contain it; so no one has power over the day
> of his death. As no one is discharged in time of war, so
> wickedness will not release those who practice it. All
> this I saw, as I applied my mind to everything done
> under the sun. There is a time when a man lords it
> over others to his own hurt (Eccles. 8:5-9).

Solomon uses subtle irony when he declares that "the wise heart will know the proper time and procedure" (v. 5). A ruler who is wise will know there is a day of reckoning (a foolish ruler will not) and so will a wise servant (or citizen or employee). For everything there is a time and a reckoning (judgment). "There is a time for everything" (3:1).

Obviously, there are limits to how far a believer can bend in obeying a ruler's commands. We have several illustrations in the Bible, probably none more vivid than those of Daniel and Peter, of people who resisted when they were pushed too far. Daniel, a young Jewish captive who had been taken to Babylon, was ordered to stop praying to God and to worship the king. He refused and was thrown into a den of lions to be killed (see Dan. 6).

When the apostle Peter was ordered by the rulers in Jerusalem to stop preaching about Jesus, he refused to obey them and declared, "We must obey God rather than men" (Acts 5:29). When the edicts of rulers or of the government or of our employers interfere with our relationship with God, we disobey them to obey God.

Certainly, our circumstances vary greatly from those Daniel and Peter experienced, and we must examine our motives and circumstances very carefully before standing against our leaders. But the principle is a scriptural one, and we ignore it to our own detriment.

Paul's letter to the Romans provides an important balance to this principle. It reminds us that God has established governmental authority for our good, and we are to obey it.

"Everyone must submit himself to the governing authorities, for there is no authority except that which God has established. The authorities that exist have been established by God. Consequently, he who rebels against the authority is rebelling against what God has instituted, and those who do so will bring judgment on themselves" (Rom. 13:1-2). God is capable of executing His own judgment; it is not our job to do so.

As a matter of principle, we are to obey the law; it is not a matter of convenience. This includes obeying the 55 miles-per-hour speed limit. I would rather drive faster. But God's Word says we are to "be subject to the governing authorities." This also includes all the other laws and ordinances provided for our benefit. "Submit yourselves for the Lord's sake to every authority instituted among men" (1 Pet. 2:13).

We are reminded that the day of death, like the day of judgment, cannot be avoided. Just as the unjust ruler cannot avoid judgment of his evil actions, so he cannot avoid his own death. "No one is discharged in time of war" (Eccles. 8:8). Wickedness may prevail in the affairs of people, but it will do no good when the time of death is at hand.

There is another irony here. "There is a time when a man lords it over another to his own hurt" (v. 9). In spite of a person's inability to rule the number of his days, he still tries to "play God" over the lives of others. The one who lords it over his subjects will have to answer to the real Lord one day! Solomon's comment that he has applied this principle "to everything done under the sun" (v. 9) shows that this is God's verdict on all who deal unjustly with those over whom they have authority. They do it to their own hurt.

How should a Christian relate to all this? Solomon has answered the question already in verse 1: We are to bless those who oppress us. Our faces are to shine upon them!

Rather than complain bitterly about our high taxes (which are low when compared to those of other Western nations), we are to "do everything without complaining or arguing, so that . . . [we] may become blameless and pure, children of God without fault in a crooked and depraved generation" (Phil. 2:14,15). What a testimony that would be!

When Life Is Unfair

If irritation with our leaders' abuses tops our list of complaints, injustice cannot be far behind. "Then too, I saw the wicked buried—those who used to come and go from the holy place and receive praise in the city where they did this. This too is meaningless.

"When the sentence for a crime is not quickly carried out, the hearts of the people are filled with schemes to do wrong. Although a wicked man commits a hundred crimes and still lives a long time, I know that it will go better with God-fearing men, who are reverent before God. Yet because the wicked do not fear God, it will not go well with them, and their days will not lengthen like a shadow.

"There is something else meaningless that occurs on earth: righteous men who get what the wicked deserve, and wicked men who get what the righteous deserve. This too, I say, is meaningless. So I commend the enjoyment of life, because nothing is better for a man under the sun than to eat and drink and be glad. Then joy will accompany him in his work all the days of the life God has given him under the sun" (Eccles. 8:10-15).

It is important to remember that the context for these verses is the wicked rulers who have lorded it over their subjects. They continue to be honored, even in death! Perhaps those who continue to praise them have gained the most from the injustices they perpetrated, and they stand to gain from the continuation of those injustices.

Solomon says, "I look at these wicked rulers who have done so many bad things to their people, and when it comes time for their funerals, they are praised in the very city where they did all their wickedness." So much for human acclaim! So much for justice!

Furthermore, because justice is not executed quickly, many people say, "Well, let's go ahead and do evil. If there was going to be any judgment, God or somebody would have done something by now!"

The psalmist struggled with the same problem: "Surely God is good to Israel, to those who are pure in heart. But as for me, my feet had almost slipped; I had nearly lost my foothold. For I envied the arrogant when I saw the prosperity of the wicked" (Ps. 73:1-3).

The psalmist goes on to talk about all the ways the wicked prosper; then he tells us he went off to worship God and was given an understanding of the actual consequences of their evil. "Surely you place them on slippery ground; you cast them down to ruin" (Ps. 73:18).

The psalmist could not understand the injustices in the world any more than we can. But he knew the character of God ("I have made the Sovereign Lord my refuge"—Ps. 73:28), and he knew that God would judge the evil ones. We can trust Him to do it, too.

It is easy to assume that because the administration of justice is slow it will never take place. It is not always possible to draw a direct line from an evil act to its judgment. Indeed, in our own time many people lament that the delay in administering justice has more to do with the breakdown of respect for the law than any other factor. Because God seems to delay His judgment, it is easy to assume that it will never come.

I remember my mother telling a story in Sunday School when I was a child. A boy who was angry with his sister took her doll and buried it in the backyard. When his sister missed it and his mother asked him if he knew where it was, he denied having anything to do with its disappearance. Months later, when the grass began to grow in the spring, the doll was outlined on the bare ground and his lie was discovered.

When I was a little boy, I enjoyed playing with matches, even though I knew better. I would find a handful of matches, take them into my parents' clothes closet, shut the door, and light them one at a time. As each match burned out, I would put it in a neat little pile in the back of the closet. I never thought about being caught, but eventually I was.

I also disliked bread crusts. I would eat the soft part of the bread and would quietly slip the crust into the little drawer on my side of the kitchen table. For the life of me, I cannot imagine how I could have thought I would get by with it.

Of course, my wrong was discovered in that instance also. When we go against God's ways, there are always a stack of matches or a drawer full of bread crusts just waiting to be discovered.

It is just a matter of time.

The injustice of evil that goes unpunished is too much for Solomon, and he returns to the theme of judgment again: "It will go better with God-fearing men . . . . It will not go well with [the wicked]" (Eccles. 8:12,13). But then he remembers the argument the secularist uses and acknowledges that this is not always true on this earth, "under the sun."

Sometimes the righteous suffer what ought to happen to the wicked, and the wicked enjoy what ought to go to the righteous. But whereas the unbeliever sees that as evidence that there is no God (or worse, even if there is one, then he is no god of mercy or is impotent), the person who lives by faith in the Lord God sees the issue differently.

Solomon has already declared, "I thought in my heart, 'God will bring to judgment both the righteous and the wicked'" (3:17). At the end of the book he proclaims, "For God will bring every deed into judgment, including every hidden thing, whether it is good or evil" (12:14). So the believer knows that God is in charge, regardless of what may be happening at the moment.

Solomon's advice is delightfully simple: "So I commend the enjoyment of life, because nothing is better for a man under the sun than to eat and drink and be glad. Then joy will accompany him in his work all the days of the life God has given him under the sun" (8:15). It is as if Solomon was saying: "You say you're all bent out of shape because injustice exists? Are you wondering if He truly loves you or if He is able to do anything about it? Don't lose any sleep over the problem. Believe me. Enjoy yourself. That's what God wants you to do. He is in charge of running the world, not you."

Was Solomon oblivious to all the troubles of humanity? Hardly. He certainly could not have written this book without knowing the score in the game of life. He was simply reminding us of what we should have known all along: God is bigger than all of these things. Yes, He will mete out judgment. Yes, evil will be punished. In the meantime, enjoy life.

Earlier in the book Solomon declared that enjoyment is from the hand of God (see 2:24,25). Then in chapter 5 he says, "Then I realized that it is good and proper for a man to eat and drink, and to find satisfaction in his toilsome labor under the sun during the few days of life which God has given him—for this is his lot" (5:18). Here he again says we should enjoy life (see 8:15). In the next chapter, he will say it again, only in the imperative case: "Go, eat your food with gladness, and drink your wine with a joyful heart" (9:7).

God made us to enjoy life, and He commands us to do so. When we see the injustices that so irritate us, we need to cease our grumbling and remember that God is the judge of all humanity (see Rom. 12:19).

When Wisdom Is Not Enough

At first glance, Solomon's advice is far too passive for our taste. It seems as if he is saying, "Well, if you can't lick 'em, join 'em." It is important to remember, however, that he has reminded us that our enjoyment of life is to be tasted alongside our work (see Eccles. 8:15). We are not to be passive, and presumably our "work" includes the pursuit of justice. Why else would God have instituted the governing authorities in the first place (see Rom. 13)? And the work of the governing authorities is done at times by Christians, too.

Solomon elaborates on his reason for advising us to enjoy our lives. We are unable to understand God's dealings, no matter how wise we are. "When I applied my mind to know wisdom and to observe man's labor on earth—his eyes not seeing sleep day or night—then I saw all that God has done. No one can comprehend what goes on under the sun. Despite all his efforts to search it out, man cannot discover its meaning. Even if a wise man claims he knows, he cannot really comprehend it" (8:16,17).

At first this seems discouraging; it is devastating to the secularist. But if we will look closely at what he is saying, we will notice that Solomon intends it to be comforting. It is, after all, the work "that God has done" that we cannot understand. It is not the work of a cosmic madman, as some would say. Nor is it the blind chance the secularist sees at work in the universe. It is God's work.

And just as the tree in the Garden of Eden stood as a reminder that God has reserved some areas of knowledge for Himself, so these verses remind us again that we shall never discover those things He has chosen to keep secret (see Deut. 29:29; Isa. 55:8,9).

All of us have inscrutible, uncomfortable experiences in our lives that we do not like and cannot understand. We read, "And we know that in all things God works for the good of those who love him, who have been called according to his purpose" (Rom. 8:28). When we read that, we sometimes wonder if it is really true.

But Solomon has told us what we need to know, and as he begins the next chapter he will review it with the words, "So I reflected on all this and concluded that the righteous and the wise and what they do are in God's hands" (Eccles. 9:1).

All that is left is to stand before Him and confess, with appropriate awe, the great affirmation of the apostle Paul in Romans 11:33-36:

> Oh, the depth of the riches of the wisdom and knowledge of God! How unsearchable his judgments, and his paths beyond tracing out! "Who has known the mind of the Lord? Or who has been his counselor?" "Who has ever given to God, that God should repay him?" For from him and through him and to him are all things. To him be the glory forever! Amen

Questions for Discussion

1. When have you felt that your vision of life was as distorted as Mr. Magoo's?
2. Do you agree with Solomon's advice concerning governmental relations? How does his advice apply to Christians who are active in the political process today?
3. When have you felt—like the psalmist—that you had almost "lost your foothold" when the wicked prospered? (See Ps. 73:1-3).
4. Do you think it is proper for Christians to "take the law into their own hands" when the administration of justice seems painfully slow? Why? Why not?
5. When in your life has wisdom been less than enough to solve a problem? What other resources did you draw upon?

CHAPTER NINE

How Can I Find Joy in a World of Death?

Ecclesiastes 9:1-9

A friend recently shared a moving experience from the first church he pastored. Armed with his textbooks and the best knowledge his professors could pour into his head, he had entered the pastorate full of enthusiasm and hope for his ministry. The answers he had learned in seminary would handle every situation he would face.

And then Sandra Anderson died.

"It devastated me," he confided. "Things like that aren't supposed to happen. She was my age, beautiful, the mother of three small children, a committed Christian and wife. The all-American woman. One night she reached across the bed to wake her husband Ralph, grabbed his shoulder violently, and then collapsed and died before he could get her to the hospital. Within minutes she had suffocated. The doctor said she had had a sudden allergic reaction to the penicillin she had been taking for a cold. Apparently, she had taken another pill only a few minutes earlier, and her body had decided it had had enough.

"I remember telling myself that this sort of thing just doesn't happen, at least not to committed people like Sandra and Ralph. The shock and desperation on Ralph's face and the confusion in their three children's eyes wouldn't leave my mind. I could hardly sleep, and I moved through all the things a pastor does at a time like that almost in a stupor.

"I was unprepared for what happened on the day of her funeral. I was a mess; but there was Ralph, comforting and encouraging the hundreds of family and neighbors and friends who had come to the funeral. It was as if he was the minister, not me.

"Later, I asked him about that day. 'How did you do it, Ralph?' I will never forget his answer.

"'The night before the funeral, I took the kids over to my sister's place. I'd held my emotions in check, but I thought I was going mad and didn't want to hurt the children anymore or have them see me kill myself or something. When I got home, I began to weep. Uncontrollably. I just couldn't stop. Finally, I managed to crawl into bed, and I lay there all night, crying and clinging to Sandra's nightgown like Linus with his blanket. I could even smell her scent on the cloth. Then, near dawn, I began to realize that I wasn't alone in the room anymore. I began to feel a peace and quiet all around me. I'd never felt anything quite like it before, and a verse of the Bible came to my mind, "Lo, I am with you alway" (Matt. 28:20, *KJV*). It was like a voice. I knew that Jesus had come into that room to comfort me, and I knew I was going to be all right.'

"Ralph paused and wiped the tears from his eyes before going on. 'I'd been as low as I think I ever could go. I'd been hurt as deeply as anything could ever hurt me. And when I touched bottom, I discovered that what you and the other pastors of this church have always said was true. There was something there I could count on. Really Someone. I could rest on something solid. And I fell asleep.'

"'And when I woke up, everything was different. Oh, I was missing Sandra and it wasn't phoney or anything. But the Lord had given me a joy I couldn't understand. That wasn't me you saw that day. I'd been filled with unspeakable joy. It was Christ. That's who you saw.'"

How *do* we find joy in a world filled with death? With cruelty and suffering on every side? How can we talk about joy in that kind of world?

Recently I viewed the film *Joni*, the moving story of the

young woman who was paralyzed from the neck down in a diving accident. Near the film's end, Joni made two profound assertions. She said there are a million questions, but only a couple of worthwhile answers. Also, there are a lot of *whys* she wonders about and does not understand, but she knows the *Who* and that's enough.

How will we face the enigmas of life? So long as we focus our attention on the *whys*, we will be disturbed by them. In the last chapter we discovered that frequently the things that happen to the "good" people should be the things that happen to the "bad" people and vice versa, and in chapter 7 we learned that sometimes adversity is good for us and prosperity is bad for us. These teachings raise at least a million questions! And the more we try to understand, the more confused we become.

Solomon has an answer to these disturbing questions: Be joyful! But he wants to be sure we get his message in all its power, and so he takes us back to the rest of his argument again. He asks the secularist to look at life very carefully. If the believer will be equally honest, there will be some insights of great value for him also.

The World Is an Enigma

It may seem strange to begin a discussion of joy in this way, but Solomon chooses to start us at the beginning of his thoughts. "So I reflected on all this and concluded that the righteous and the wise and what they do are in God's hands, but no man knows whether love or hate awaits him" (9:1).

According to the witness of Scripture, we should be able to see the hand of a mighty Creator in nature (see Ps. 19; Rom. 1:18-32). Even so, we have no objective way of knowing His attitude toward us: "no man knows whether love or hate awaits him" (Eccles. 9:1).

It is important to remember that Solomon is speaking from our perspective, that of the mortal. The one who lives "under the sun" is unable to tell by anything observable whether the God who made the sun is a God of love or hate.

Solomon has already made the point that the secular mind

cannot be honest and come to any conclusion about life other than despair. Now he rubs it in. He says, "You don't even know what kind of a world this is, and you never will!" So long as people limit themselves to what they can observe—"by anything that is before them"—they will never understand the works of God.

But Solomon also said that "the righteous and the wise and what they do are in God's hands (9:1). That is, God *is* a God of love, and He is in control.

People may not know this by what they observe in the world at large, but it is important to know that it is true. The believer—who has been made God's righteousness (see 2 Cor. 5:21)—can understand this, but the unbeliever cannot be consistent with his own "faith" and believe it. So these words—again—have a different meaning for the Christian than they have for the unbeliever. They are no cause for despair; God is known and His character is well-attested!

Solomon has already explained that we do not have the power to know what is good for us or what is evil (see Eccles. 8:17). Here Solomon's words remind us that we do not know whether the things which come to us are God's blessing or His judgment. They could be either. There are times when it seems as if God is judging us, but the truth is that He has allowed it so that some good will take place in our lives.

Of course, it could be judgment, too! We do reap what we sow, and sometimes we simply suffer for our sin or stupidity. There is not much joy in that kind of suffering. It is foolish to step back and say, "I'm pressing on to higher ground," when we just dug ourselves a pit and fell into it!

But even in judgment God does not leave us. He teaches and corrects us. And in all troubled times there are lessons to learn. James wrote, "Consider it pure joy, my brothers, whenever you face trials of many kinds" (James 1:2). Why? "The testing of your faith develops perseverance. Perseverance must finish its work so that you may be mature and complete, not lacking anything" (James 1:3-4). You see, God's ways are inscrutable. Sometimes we say, "Ah, now I know why such and such happened." But we probably do not! At best we see only a small fraction of God's purposes. Trials come for many reasons, and it is presumptuous for us to think we know more than we do.

Remember the story of Hosea. God told him to marry an immoral woman who was repeatedly unfaithful to him. Surely Hosea suffered greatly because of his wife's sin. But God commanded this so that Hosea might know how the Lord felt about the spiritual harlotry of Israel and might declare it with power and conviction. Hosea learned something, and the result was that the people were called to repentance.

On one occasion Jesus and His disciples came upon a man who had been blind from birth. Believing that such an unfortunate condition had to be a direct consequence of sin, they asked Him whether this man or his parents had committed a great sin. Jesus' comment was that neither case was true; it happened for the glory of God (see John 9:1-3). We, too, most likely have troubles that come our way so that God can be glorified. Do we allow them to glorify Him?

God wants us to grow, to stretch. He wants us to sink our roots deeper. It is in the time of drought that the plant sinks its roots farther into the soil. So it is with us.

Sometimes God wants us to suffer. We are called to suffer with Him: "But rejoice that you participate in the sufferings of Christ, so that you may be overjoyed when his glory is revealed" (1 Pet. 4:13). We are to know "the fellowship of sharing in his sufferings" (Phil. 3:10).

Granted, Christians in the United States do not suffer persecution as did the Christians of the early church and as Christians in Uganda, Cambodia, Viet Nam, Latin America, and numerous other countries suffer today. But I believe God designs special sufferings for each one of us so that we can grow in those areas that only these special sufferings allow.

But life is not filled only with enigmas and suffering. There is much more.

Life Is Worth Living

We may not realize it while we are experiencing life's enigmas, but life is definitely of great value.

All share a common destiny—the righteous and the
wicked, the good and the bad, the clean and the
unclean, those who offer sacrifices and those who do
not. As it is with the good man, so with the sinner; as
it is with those who take oaths, so with those who are
afraid to take them. This is the evil in everything that
happens under the sun: The same destiny overtakes
all. The hearts of men, moreover, are full of evil and
there is madness in their hearts while they live, and
afterward they join the dead. Anyone who is among
the living has hope—even a live dog is better off than
a dead lion! For the living know that they will die, but
the dead know nothing; they have no further reward,
and even the memory of them is forgotten. Their love,
their hate and their jealousy have long since vanished;
never again will they have a part in anything that happens under the sun (Eccles. 9:2-6).

"All share a common destiny" (v. 2). We all die. As far as the
secularist is concerned, death is serious business. On the other
hand, life is of inestimable value. It is so valuable that anything is
better than death. "Anyone who is among the living has hope—
even a live dog is better off than a dead lion" (9:4). In those days
a dog was considered a despicable creature (see 1 Sam. 17:43;
24:14). The lion, however, has always been viewed as a beast of
power, majesty, and grandeur.

Solomon was not giving advice on how to choose a household
pet. He was simply saying that he would rather be a live dog—
despicable as it was considered—than a dead lion—"the king of
the jungle." Better to live than to die? Why? Because there is
hope for the living. We have a similar expression: "Where there's
life, there's hope." Life is precious. There need be no other reason.

But there is.

While there is life, there is a chance to prepare for death.
There is a time to prepare to meet God. And when we die, there
are no more opportunities to do anything worthwhile on earth.

Solomon is talking about mortal humans and mortal life. Eternity is not in view when he says:

> For the living know that they will die, but the dead
> know nothing; they have no further reward, and even
> the memory of them is forgotten. Their love, their
> hate and their jealousy have long since vanished
> (Eccles. 9:5,6).

He is talking about life "under the sun," life here and now. It is valuable; it is worth living.

Life Is a Cause for Joy

The ability to enjoy life is a *gift* to believers (see 2:25,26). It is not a possibility for unbelievers. It is sad that so often those who have the gift for enjoying life forget to use it. Yes, life has its enigmas, but we are commanded to enjoy it.

> Go, eat your food with gladness, and drink your wine
> with a joyful heart, for it is now that God favors what
> you do. Always be clothed in white, and always anoint
> your head with oil. Enjoy life with your wife, whom
> you love, all the days of this meaningless life that God
> has given you under the sun—all your meaningless
> days. For this is your lot in life and in your toilsome
> labor under the sun (9:7-9).

Notice the progression. In chapter 2, verses 24-26, Solomon recommends that we enjoy life. In chapter 3, verse 12, he says it again. In chapter 5, verse 18, he tells us it is our heritage. In chapter 8, verse 15, he commands that we enjoy life, and here again in chapter 9 he tells us, "Live joyfully."

When Solomon speaks of bread and wine, he is talking about the staple diet of the time, a plain meal. We might say "meat and potatoes." The point is that we are to receive even the humble things in life with joy, not just the special things.

We have a simple rule at our house: We seldom take on

heavy subjects while we are eating. We do not talk about the bills that are due, the energy crisis, the political scene, any discipline or correction that needs to take place in our family, or problems from the church. We have the rest of the day to deal with those subjects. Meals are our time for positive, affirming, upbuilding talk—or silence. It is one way we try to communicate the joy of life to our children. Sometimes we parents have to go out of our way to make the point.

Not long ago I was speaking out of town, and a man I have known for 20 years came bounding up to me. "Bob," he exclaimed, "isn't it great how the Lord keeps us young and happy and rejoicing!" With an attitude like that, you might think he had the world by the tail. Not at all. For one thing, I wouldn't have his job for anything. I found myself warmed by his enthusiasm and love for the Lord as we talked, and I am convinced that his words did at least as much for me that day as mine did for him.

Do you know how to exude joy? Or do you concentrate on problems?

When Solomon refers to white garments and a well-oiled head, he is speaking of celebration—of a party. In those days the ordinary person wore cool, white garments for festive occasions only. He could not afford to keep them crisp and clean like the wealthy, who wore their white robes far more regularly. So the picture he paints is one of real rejoicing, a constant festive occasion. God wants our lives to be like a joyful party.

Even though he failed miserably in this area himself, Solomon tells us that it is important for us to build joyful marriages. It is a part of what God intends for us to enjoy. We are not to become so enamored with our activities and work—including that which we do for the Lord—that we neglect the love of our youth. It is so important to nurture that love, to cultivate and enjoy that relationship. It is part of our portion in life. It is what God wants for us, and it should be one of the real highlights of daily life.

The price for a good marriage must be paid every day. There's an even higher price to pay when we will not pay the price to make marriage good.

We have not been given the answer to every question we can ask. There always will be enigmas, and in many cases we never will know the answers. But we are to refuse to allow them to rob us of the joy God wants us to have. "This is the day the Lord has made; let us rejoice and be glad in it" (Ps. 118:24). "The joy of the Lord is your strength" (Neh. 8:10).

Let us be sure that these words of Scripture become rooted deep in our souls.

Questions for Discussion

1. In your opinion, why is life worth living?
2. If a friend asked your advice on how to prepare for death, what would you say?
3. James 1:3 says that "the testing of your faith develops perseverance." When have you seen this verse proven true? What other qualities have trials and testing developed in your life or the lives of people you know?
4. God has given you the ability to enjoy life. How have you used the gift in the past week? To what extent is the enjoyment of life a conscious choice?

CHAPTER TEN

How Should I Approach My Work?

Ecclesiastes 9:10–11:6

When life is over, what have I gained? What is my profit? Solomon personally faced these questions as he wrote the book of Ecclesiastes. In the process of looking at life, he has shown us that we will not find satisfaction in knowledge, pleasure, or achievement—places where we normally look for it. Neither is it to be found in hard work or in wealth.

Life is full of harsh realities—injustice, death, oppression. It is filled with enigmas; we cannot really know whether something that happens to us is for good or for bad. What we feel is bad or unfair may turn out to be the best thing that ever happend to us.

So what shall we do? Do we give up? Do we become passive? Do we just go through the motions, doing enough to look good but not really having our hearts in it?

Work Energetically Even if the Results Are Uncertain

When the granddaughter of the great conductor, Arturo Toscanini, was interviewed a few years ago, she was asked to identify the most important thing in her grandfather's life. Her response was surprising: Whatever he was doing at the moment! She went on to add that this was true whether he was peeling an orange or conducting a great symphony. The *important* thing was the thing he was doing.

Of course we can't all be Arturo Toscaninis, but regardless of our station in life, Solomon has provided us with valuable insights into our work—the tasks and concerns to which we give our energy, not just those things for which we are paid. Some of what he has to say is very clear and logical, while some of it is in loose collections of wise sayings, much as in the Proverbs.

> Whatever your hand finds to do, do it with all your might, for in the grave, where you are going, there is neither working nor planning nor knowledge nor wisdom. I have seen something else under the sun: The race is not to the swift or the battle to the strong, nor does food come to the wise or wealth to the brilliant or favor to the learned; but time and chance happen to them all. Moreover, no man knows when his hour will come: As fish are caught in a cruel net, or birds are taken in a snare, so men are trapped by evil times that fall unexpectedly upon them (Eccles. 9:10-12).

We are to do what we do with our "might," whether it is peeling an orange or directing a symphony, scrubbing floors or directing a corporation. Whatever our tasks, we are to do them as unto the Lord. Colossians 3:23 says something very similar: "Whatever you do, work at it with all your heart, as working for the Lord, not for men." This precludes the excuse, "Oh, if I were working for the Lord, it would be different. But where I work, it doesn't make any difference."

It does.

We are to serve God in everything we do. Granted, while we serve the Lord, we do serve people, too; but we must always remember that our real loyalty is to the Lord. We work enthusiastically, not as unto others, but as unto the Lord. When we help the Red Cross or the Girl Scouts, we are to do it as unto the Lord.

Someone has said, "Doing a little thing for God makes it a big thing." So, "Whatever your hand finds to do, do it with all your might" (Eccles. 9:10). Do it with energy! Do it with enthusiasm! It was Thoreau who said, "None are so old as those who have outlived enthusiasm." He was right.

Solomon has already told us that life brings forces beyond our control to bear upon us (see 3:1-8). We have only one life to make our contribution; where we are going, there will be "neither working nor planning nor knowledge nor wisdom" (9:10). But in verses 11 and 12 we begin to see the effects of both time and chance.

The fastest runner is not always the one who wins the race; the strongest warrior does not always win the battle (v. 11). Solomon could have had Samson in mind. Who was a mightier warrior than he, and yet who ever lost more? (His story is told in Judges 13–16.)

Solomon could also have had his own father, David, in mind. When David was still a young man, he confronted the Philistine giant Goliath and declared, "You come against me with sword and spear and javelin, but I come against you in the name of the Lord Almighty" (1 Sam. 17:45). Who won? David, of course.

David's friend Jonathan faced the Philistines with only a handful of soldiers. As he led them into battle he declared, "Nothing can hinder the Lord from saving, whether by many or by few" (1 Sam. 14:6). The prophet Jeremiah explained why these apparent "upsets" in the natural order of things happen: "It is not for man to direct his steps" (Jer. 10:23).

God Is in Control, Not Humanity

Solomon has listed five assets that ought to guarantee success—speed, strength, wisdom, intelligence, skill. We would think that those who are quick, those who are strong, those who are wise, those who have intelligence, and those who know how to do things best would be the winners in life. Solomon says, "No, not necessarily. We do not direct our own steps. There is a higher power—God."

The psalmist wrote that the 'person who walks with the Lord, who meditates on His Word, will be like the "tree planted by streams of water . . . . Whatever he does prospers" (Ps. 1:3). The Scriptures repeatedly declare that it is God who makes us prosper (see Gen. 39:3, 23; Deut. 29:9; 1 Kings 22:15; 2 Chron. 26:5; Neh. 2:20; Ps. 122:6).

So far as work is concerned, the results are not always certain. We do not know which races we will win and which battles we will be triumphant in. But God is at work; and because He is the one who directs our steps, we ought to work with enthusiasm.

When Solomon ends his comments about the five assets that may turn out to be of little value, he says, "but time and chance happen to them all" (Eccles. 9:11). No matter how much ability we have, time and chance take their toll.

Most of us are convinced that the opposite is true. We believe we are the masters of our fates, the captains of our souls. The secular mind is particularly insistent on this very point. "Not so," says Solomon. "Moreover, no man knows when his hour will come: As fish are caught in a cruel net, or birds are taken in a snare, so men are trapped by evil times that fall unexpectedly upon them" (9:12).

Rather than the masters of our fates, humanity is more like a little fish. We swim along minding our own business, and suddenly we are snatched up by a net. There is nothing we can do about it. That image is the correct comparison for our lives, not this silly, vain talk about being masters and captains.

What will we do if a heart or lung fails us? What can we do if we contract a fatal disease? Not one thing! What can we do if we lose our jobs or our businesses? What will we do if a child dies or our spouses leave us? How many times I have seen someone going along so well, and then—like a net scooping up a fish—it was all over.

Time and chance happen to everyone. We cannot predict what will happen to us or when it might occur. But regardless, we are to work with all our might. Solomon says, "Look, give it your best shot. Work with enthusiasm."

Ability is not as important as availability!

Work with the Benefit of Wisdom

In another book Solomon wrote, "The fear of the Lord is the beginning of knowledge" (Prov. 1:7), and the epistle of James reads, "If any of you lacks wisdom, he should ask God" (James 1:5). Wisdom is a gift; God gives it. It is the ability to see things as God sees them. While we are to work with enthusiasm, we are also to work with wisdom.

> I also saw under the sun this example of wisdom that greatly impressed me: There was once a small city with only a few people in it. And a powerful king came against it, surrounded it and built huge siegeworks against it.
> Now there lived in that city a man poor but wise, and he saved the city by his wisdom. But nobody remembered that poor man. So I said, "Wisdom is better than strength." But the poor man's wisdom is despised, and his words are no longer heeded. The quiet words of the wise are more to be heeded than the shouts of a ruler of fools. Wisdom is better than weapons of war, but one sinner destroys much good (Eccles. 9:13-18).

At first glance it appears as if Solomon is saying it is foolish to be wise. A wise man delivers a city, but he is quickly forgotten and passes into oblivion. His point is that this is the gratitude one can expect for wisdom—it frequently goes unrewarded. It is good to realize that before we ask for it!

When Solomon declares, "Wisdom is better than weapons of war, but one sinner destroys much good" (9:18), he reminds us how valuable and vulnerable wisdom is. Wars could be avoided if we would live by wisdom, and it takes very little folly to destroy the fruits of wisdom.

This holds true in the arena of personal morality as much as in politics; how many have ruined their lives or reputations by one foolish action! The phrase, "One sinner destroys much good," is like our, "One rotten apple ruins the whole barrel."

Why? The god of this world is Satan, and even a small effort from a sinner is met with an enthusiastic response.

Solomon amplifies these ideas in the following verses:

> As dead flies give perfume a bad smell, so a little folly
> outweighs wisdom and honor. The heart of the wise
> inclines to the right, but the heart of the fool to the
> left. Even as he walks along the road, the fool lacks
> sense and shows everyone how stupid he is (10:1-3).

It is easier to raise a stink than to create something beautiful! Some people seem to feel called to create problems. Their "little folly" frequently does far more damage than the good of many.

Verse two is not a political statement! Solomon simply says, "The heart of the wise inclines to the right." *Left* and *right* are figurative expressions for "wrong" and "right," just as Jesus used the words *sheep* and *goats* to speak of those who follow Him and those who do not (Matt. 25:32).

Furthermore, the one distinguishing mark of the fool is that he cannot disguise what he is (see Eccles. 10:3). His actions and his words—indeed, everything about him—show him to be the fool he is.

The wisdom literature of the Bible frequently comments on the fool. The book of Proverbs speaks of him in many ways: Even when he says something right, it sounds wrong (see 17:7); it is wiser to avoid him (see 17:12); he loves to talk but does not listen (see 18:2); he is likely to cause conflict wherever he goes (see 18:6,7); his meddlesomeness is the cause of quarreling (see 20:3); honor does not fit his character (see 26:1); he is undependable (see 26:6,7). "Even a fool who keeps silent is considered wise; when he closes his lips, he is deemed intelligent" (17:28 *RSV*).

We have a similar expression, "Better to be thought a fool than to open your mouth and prove it."

We Are to Exercise Self-Control

Solomon moves on to speak of our relationships with those

with whom we work. His words apply equally well to our bosses as to the political authorities.

> If a ruler's anger rises against you, do not leave your post; calmness can lay great errors to rest. There is an evil I have seen under the sun, the sort of error that arises from a ruler: Fools are put in many high positions, while the rich occupy the low ones. I have seen slaves on horseback, while princes go on foot like slaves (Eccles. 10:4-7).

The reason we are to be submissive to an unfair master is that his anger may be calmed by our own wise behavior. There is no benefit to be had in the anger of *two* people. Earlier, Solomon has written, "Through patience a ruler can be persuaded" (Prov. 25:15) and "A gentle answer turns away wrath, but a harsh word stirs up anger" (Prov. 15:1). When one person is angry, the calm of another may restore a peaceable relationship. It works!

Furthermore, there is value in stable relationships. The reference in Ecclesiastes 10:7 to servants riding on horses and princes walking where servants would be expected to walk makes this very point. When errors of judgment are made, those who are inexperienced or incompetent are often admitted to positions of responsibility beyond their abilities; and everyone suffers. So when we are offended, we would be wise to swallow our pride and continue our work. If we indulge our self-righteousness and abandon our work, those who replace us may do a great deal of damage.

Work with Wisdom

Solomon then proceeds to describe five situations in which wisdom has run amok and hurt has resulted from foolish actions:

> Whoever digs a pit may fall into it; whoever breaks through a wall may be bitten by a snake. Whoever

quarries stones may be injured by them; whoever
splits logs may be endangered by them. If the ax is
dull and its edge unsharpened, more strength is
needed but skill will bring success (10:8-10).

We ought to work with wisdom. The theme of the pit's
becoming a trap to its maker is repeated frequently in Scripture
(Ps. 7:15; 9:15; 35:7,8; 57:6; Prov. 26:27; 28:10).

The comment about the serpent's biting the one who leans
against the wall (see also Amos 5:19) would be humorous in that
culture. Since the walls were made of stones and everyone
knew that snakes enjoy the cool shade and crevices that go with
a stone wall, only a fool would casually lean against one without
first checking it for snakes.

Furthermore, the careless person who quarries stones can
easily be injured, and the one who splits wood carelessly can
injure himself with the ax. Finally, the man who tries to cut wood
with a dull ax has no one to blame for his misery but himself. He
could make his work much easier, but instead he uses the dull
blade and has to work much harder than necessary.

So wisdom is the difference between success and failure in
our work. If we want success, we must use our God-given intelligence and do our work God's way.

Let Your Words Glorify God

If a snake bites before it is charmed, there is no profit
for the charmer. Words from a wise man's mouth are
gracious, but a fool is consumed by his own lips. At
the beginning his words are folly; at the end they are
wicked madness—and the fool multiplies words. No
one knows what is coming—who can tell him what will
happen after him? A fool's work wearies him; he does
not know the way to town (Eccles. 10:11-15).

In the first three lines of this Scripture passage, Solomon
warns against stirring up "the babbler," the gossip, whom he

compares to a dangerous snake. We all have known someone with a venomous tongue, and we know the damage loose talk can do. Solomon admonishes us to be circumspect in our speech when talking to such a person, lest we give him more fuel for his fire.

In contrast, think of the people you know with whom it is a blessing to talk. Their words are kind and helpful, winsome and warm. That kind of person's words help him; they are gracious. But a fool's words destroy him. He may appear as if he is doing all right until he speaks; then he reveals who he is and he's in trouble.

The fool's problem is not that he is slow-witted; one could hardly blame a person who is handicapped with low intelligence for his problem. No, the problem of the fool is that he thinks wrongly; he refuses to begin with God. Solomon says that "at the beginning his words are folly" (v. 13); he has chosen to reject God, a judgment that should bring consternation to the secularist.

Solomon's point is that the one who lives without God does so deliberately. He has *chosen* to do so; he did not make his decision purely on the basis of objective evidence.

One writer comments, "If there are innumerable unbelievers whose earthly end could hardly be described as either wickedness or madness, it is only because the logic of their unbelief has not been followed through, thanks to the restraining grace of God."[1]

We already have seen that nobody knows what the future will bring (see 3:22; 6:12; 7:14; 8:7), but that does not deter the fool (10:14). He will tell you what will happen, and in detail! Never mind the fact that he has even less reason to know than those to whom he speaks.

The comment in verse 15 is priceless: "A fool's work wearies him; he does not know the way to town." The fool is the kind of person who would get lost on an airplane! His whole orientation to life is so wrong that even ignorance cannot account for it; he contrives his lostness. He would make a straight road crooked; and even if he managed by chance to stumble upon the city, he would find a way to get lost in it!

A Word to the Wise

Solomon has one final word to say about living and working wisely:

> Woe to you, O land whose king was a servant and
> whose princes feast in the morning. Blessed are you,
> O land whose king is of noble birth and whose princes
> eat at a proper time—for strength and not for drunk-
> enness. If a man is lazy, the rafters sag; if his hands
> are idle, the house leaks. A feast is made for laughter,
> and wine makes life merry, but money is the answer
> for everything. Do not revile the king even in your
> thoughts, or curse the rich in your bedroom, because
> a bird of the air may carry your words, and a bird on
> the wing may report what you say (10:16-20).

We are affected by the tone set by those at the top of any organization. This is true of both good and bad leaders. Laziness, incompetence, or moral failure in any organization will cause it to collapse. This is true of nations, businesses, families. The word *servant* in verse 16 may literally refer to a youthful leader, or it may refer to one who has gained a position of authority without accepting its responsibility. Either way, when an immature person rules an organization, it will be in trouble soon.

Solomon summarizes the philosophy of the childlike leader in verse 19: "A feast is made for laughter, and wine makes life merry; but money is the answer for everything." A fitting slogan for a fool!

The practical question is, "What shall I do when my boss is a fool?" Solomon warns us against stirring up opposition (see v. 20); a true fool will likely be vindictive, and those who have reached high places often have a sixth sense for knowing who their enemies are.

Recently, a friend who lived near Uganda during the rule of Idi Amin—its insane, cruel dictator—told me that Amin had a sense for knowing how to escape danger. Several attempts were made on his life, and each time he sensed something was wrong and took unusual precautions. Even at the end he managed to escape with his life.

The fool may be foolish, but he has a real knack for survival, warns Solomon. Be wise. Do your work well and wisely. Don't even think bad thoughts about your leaders.

Be gracious in your words. Work intelligently and wisely. Keep wisdom with you in all your work.

Work Actively Even if Conditions Are Uncertain

As we work, it is wise to remember the realities of chapter 9, verses 11 and 12. We have no guarantees; time and chance can alter our best plans and destroy everything. While this is a disaster for the secularist, Solomon also intends for it to serve as a call to action for the believer. Since we have no guarantees for the future, it is better to risk following the Lord than to play it safe and withdraw from the activities of life.

> Cast your bread upon the waters, for after many days
> you will find it again. Give portions to seven, yes to
> eight, for you do not know what disaster may come
> upon the land (11:1,2).

This is simply good advice; it makes sense. Since we cannot know when we will need help, it is wise to use our generosity to make as many friends as possible. Is this selfish? Not necessarily. If everyone would cast his "bread upon the waters," we would not need welfare or Social Security or any of the other expensive government programs that force us to do what we should gladly do on our own.

These words strike me as being very similar to Jesus' own words: "With the measure you use, it will be measured to you" (Matt 7:2, see also Mark 4:24; Luke 6:38). "Whoever finds his life will lose it, and whoever loses his life for my sake will find it" (Matt. 10:39; see also Luke 14:26; John 12:25).

This is a good way to work. It is a good way to live.

We ought to help those in need. I frequently hear people

complain about those in need—the boat people, the poor, transients. "They're lazy. Those foreigners will go on welfare if we bring them over here." "If we send food over there, the Russians may get hold of it and put their stamp on the packages." I would rather try to feed the hungry than worry about all the abuses that might happen and not try to feed them.

We comfortable North Americans have become so insulated from the sufferings of people in other parts of the world that we fail to see the face of Christ in those who suffer. Instead, we think of the political advantages or disadvantages of helping them. It would be "better" to let the politicians—whose job it is to worry about politics—and the secularists—who really have no reason to help anyone in the first place—worry about all the reasons not to help those in need.

I have almost shuddered in my soul when Christians have been critical of feeding the hungry and destitute while we bring the gospel to them. When I hear those complaints, I frequently think of Solomon's words, "If a man shuts his ears to the cry of the poor, he too will cry out and not be answered" (Prov. 21:13). We need to get busy feeding the hungry and clothing the naked and comforting the suffering.

Someday the tables could be turned.

Redeem the Time

If clouds are full of water, they pour rain upon the earth. Whether a tree falls to the south or to the north, in the place where it falls, there will it lie. Whoever watches the wind will not plant; whoever looks at the clouds will not reap (Eccles. 11:3,4).

We need to distinguish between those things about which we can do nothing and those about which we can. We cannot stop nature's patterns; the rain will fall where it will, and the tree will fall where it will, too.

But we do not have to be passive. Solomon is saying, "So what if it isn't an ideal day to sow, and so what if it isn't an ideal day to reap? If you wait for everything to be perfect, you will never do anything."

Our task in life is to deal with its realities the best we can. The conditions always could be better; but it is "better" for us to do our best with what we have than to wait for the perfect conditions, which may never come.

Confidence Is A Product of Faith

> As you do not know the path of the wind, or how the
> body is formed in a mother's womb, so you cannot
> understand the work of God, the Maker of all things.
> Sow your seed in the morning, and at evening let not
> your hands be idle, for you do not know which will
> succeed, whether this or that, or whether both will do
> equally well (11:5,6).

Finally, Solomon tells us why we can work with confidence in the midst of uncertainty. Those uncertain circumstances are in the hands "of God, the Maker of all things" (v. 5). He not only created the physical world—the wind that blows—He also created humanity—the child that grows in its mother's womb.

This is the reason we should move ahead with our work (and by "work" I mean everything that occupies our creative and productive attention, not just our occupations). We do not know the consequences of the opportunities that come our way. We are not to wait until we know the results of our work before we take action, and we ought not be content to stay unemployed until the "perfect" job falls into our lap. Both are good formulas for failure. Rather, we are to get on with it. The work is ours; the result is God's.

The Scriptures say we are to redeem the time "because the days are evil" (Eph. 5:16). We do not know which of our actions will prosper and which will fail. Furthermore, even when we think something is a failure, it may actually be a success; and when we think something is a success, it may have been a failure (see Eccles. 6:12).

A man recently told me of a friend of his whose commitment to the Lord was rather halfhearted. As they discussed their professions one day, his friend said, "Man, in my business the only thing that counts is profit. The only question I ask in getting into a deal is whether I can make a buck, and the faster the better."

My friend asked him if as a Christian he really believed that, but he did not push the point.

Several months later, his friend called him on the telephone and made an appointment for lunch. As they ate, he told an inspiring story. "You know, Ron, the craziest thing happened to me recently. I thought about that conversation we had several months ago and decided I would show you just how wrong you were and how stupid your question was. So I looked for the right opportunity to practice 'Christian love' in the business world.

"Sure enough, about a month-and-a-half ago I had a guy over the barrel. He had taken a gamble and had lost, and I could have forced him to live up to the letter of our agreement. Well, I wasn't real self-righteous about it or anything; but I explained that I had values other than just making an easy buck, and then I let him off the hook. It cost me about 20 thousand dollars off the bottom line to do it, but I gave him a break.

"You want to know something really crazy? I'd never been able to work with that guy. I couldn't even stand him. But in the last month he has given me more business than in the last five years, and I'm over a 100 thousand to the good even counting the 20 I lost. We've even become friends."

We are told in the Scriptures to love our neighbors, to witness about Jesus Christ, to raise our children to love and fear the Lord, to be loyal and honest employees and employers, to give generously to those in need, as well as many other commands. We are not to wait for the ideal circumstances to begin to obey these commands. We are not to wait until their "success" is guaranteed, as though we are wise enough to know what success would be.

We are to get on with it.

"Whatever your hand finds to do, do it with all your might" (9:10). Do it with energy. Do it with wisdom.

But do it.

Note
1. Derek Kidner, *A Time to Mourn, and a Time to Dance* (Downer's Grove, IL: Inter-Varsity Press, 1976), p. 92.

Questions for Discussion

1. Someone once said, "Any work done by a Christian is work done unto the Lord." What light does this statement shed on your daily tasks? What must you do to insure that the work you do is "done unto the Lord"?
2. Solomon asserts that time and chance affect us all. Yet, Paul, in Romans 8:28, proclaimed that *God* works all things for our good. Do you find these two thoughts compatible? Why? Why not?
3. Based on Ecclesiastes 10:4-7, what advice would you give to a friend who finds it difficult to submit to an unfair employer?
4. When do you find it most difficult to glorify God with your words? Have you spoken words this week that you wish you had never said? What will you do to heal the wounds that your words may have caused?
5. What opportunities do you have today to help needy people? Will you act on these opportunities?

CHAPTER ELEVEN

How Can I Get the Most Out of My Life?

Ecclesiastes 11:7–12:7

Once we have explored the questions that matter, what profit is there? (see 1:3). This is the question Solomon repeatedly asks throughout the book of Ecclesiastes. What profit is there in my life?

As we have looked at life with Solomon's assistance, we have seen that we do not find gain in the places people normally expect to find it. The reality of death changes every question; ultimately, there is no gain for us "under the sun." If there is to be any profit, it will have to come from something other than what we see. It will have to be a gift from God.

Interestingly enough, Solomon makes it a point several times to say, "Be sure you enjoy your life. That is what God wants for you, even though it has its limits and ultimately ends in death." Furthermore, "He has made everything beautiful in its time" (3:11). Everything fits together in God's plan—birth and death, happiness and sorrow, celebrating and mourning, gaining and losing. "He has also set eternity in the hearts of men; yet they cannot fathom what God has done from beginning to end" (3:11). We are pilgrims in this life, and we do not know all the answers to the questions we ask.

I am frequently asked by someone who is suffering, "Why do you think this happened?" I can only guess at the reasons and can truthfully answer, "Just like you, I don't know. But I know who does, and that's enough for me." He is a God of infinite, unending love. We can trust Him.

So we come through life with perhaps a million questions and only a couple of worthwhile answers, but they are enough. Who is in charge? God. What is He like? He's like a love beyond our fondest hopes! I rejoice in those two answers. I live in them by faith and hope.

It is from this perspective, then, that we should study Solomon's final words. We need to keep our eyes sharp and our hearts soft as we look for what God is saying through them.

Enjoy the Present with an Eye to the Future

It is not easy for us to enjoy the present. When we are young, we tend to look forward to the future and say, "Oh, I wonder what it will be like! I'm really going to enjoy my life when I get older!" When we are older, it is tempting to look back on our earlier years and say, "Ah, those were the good old days! How good they were, but how I wish I had put them to better use!" God doesn't want us to dwell on the past or only daydream about the future; He wants us to find joy—through Him—in the present. So Solomon tells us, "Enjoy your life, but keep your eye on the future."

Light is sweet, and it pleases the eyes to see the sun.
However many years a man may live, let him enjoy
them all. But let him remember the days of darkness,
for they will be many. Everything to come is meaningless. Be happy, young man, while you are young, and
let your heart give you joy in the days of your youth.
Follow the ways of your heart and whatever your eyes
see, but know that for all these things God will bring
you to judgment. So then, banish anxiety from your
heart and cast off the troubles of your body, for youth
and vigor are meaningless (11:7-10).

Life is both delightful and serious. Its delights will last as long as we live, but not one moment longer. In the Scripture, "light" often is a synonym for "life." Its sweetness is to be enjoyed. When we are dead, we can no longer see the sun. That is, we will no longer enjoy "life under the sun."

We are to enjoy all our days, regardless of our age. But we are also to remember that the days of death—*darkness* is an image here for death—will be many. Death ushers us into eternity, and eternity is much longer than the few short years of our lives.

Solomon has wise advice for us in the days of our youth— enjoy yourself! He tells us to enjoy all the pleasures we can, but to remember that true joy will come from doing what is right. "But know that for all these things God will bring you to judgment" (v. 9). The only thing God wants to take from us is emptiness, "vanity!"

Solomon is saying, "Live your life to the full. Enjoy your youth and get all the real joy you can. Just be sure to remember that someday you will give account of yourself to God. So pursue the innocent joys—the pure, godly, wholesome joys." The world will try to convince us that we are missing out on something, but we need to realize that the only things God would withhold from us are not worthwhile. Indeed, when we limit ourselves to the joys that are wholesome, we are free to do the things that actually bring joy, instead of guilt or regret. That lesson applies as well to adults as it does to youth.

When Solomon says, "Banish anxiety from your heart," he is telling us not to dread the loss of our youth while we should be enjoying it. It would be a disaster to miss the joy of our youth by fretting that some day we will no longer be young. Granted, the prospect of aging is terrifying for the secularist; but the Christian can see that every stage of life fits into God's good plan. It is good to be 40! So we are to live life to its full and live godly, holy lives.

Live for Your Creator During Your Strongest Days

This point grows quite naturally out of the first one. If we are going to live joyful, wholesome lives, then we ought to get busy now, while we have our greatest potential for joy.

> Remember your Creator in the days of your youth,
> before the days of trouble come and the years
> approach when you will say, "I find no pleasure in
> them"—before the sun and the light and the moon and
> the stars grow dark, and the clouds return after the
> rain (12:1,2).

To "remember" does not mean not to forget, or to jog one's memory. It is more like the story of God's remembering Hannah in chapter 1 of 1 Samuel. Hannah was barren and suffered tremendous embarrassment over it. Finally, in desperation she prayed for a child, and "the Lord remembered her" (1 Sam. 1:19).

Does this mean that God had been so preoccupied with something else that He had forgotten about Hannah's problem? No. It means He acted decisively on her behalf. When we "remember" God, we act decisively on His behalf; and when Solomon tells us to remember the Lord while we are young, he is telling us to consciously commit ourselves to serving Him. It is as if he is saying: "Begin to serve Him while you are enjoying your life. Give your life to Him right now. Don't wait."

Live for your Creator during your strongest days!

The "difficult days" that come speak of the natural process of aging, in which our bodies begin to creak and groan and fall apart. It is amazing how quickly those days come! Someone said that getting older happens fast. "About the time your face clears up your mind gets fuzzy." Before we get to the stage where we say, "Boy, life sure isn't as much fun as it used to be," we ought to set our minds toward serving God with the best years of our lives. Through Solomon, God is saying, "Give me everything now. You will enjoy life more if you do, and you will be glad you did."

When he turns to describing the infirmities of old age, Solomon's words take on a somber tone. "The sun and the light and the moon and the stars" (Eccles. 12:2) are all symbolic of joy. Our Creator wants us to delight in Him during the carefree days of our youth—the days before "the clouds return after the rain" (v. 2). He contrasts this stage of life with the "difficult days" of infirmity and old age, when one trouble comes upon the heels of another.

When we are young, we have the strength and resilience to overcome trouble; in our old age we will need every bit of strength we can find. It is better to face this while we are young and get on with living for God than it is to wait until all our strength is taken up with surviving and there is none left for serving the Lord.

Remember God in Your Last Days

Verses 3-6 present an allegory in which Solomon compares an old, dilapidated house to our bodies as we age. He is not saying that all of these things happen to everybody. But it is an allegory that fittingly describes what we can expect in old age; and it should motivate us to serve God in our youth, whether our "youth" means our teens and twenties, or the "youth" of whatever years are left.

When the keepers of the house tremble, and the
strong men stoop, when the grinders cease because
they are few, and those looking through the windows
grow dim, when the doors to the street are closed and
the sound of grinding fades; when men rise up at the
sound of birds, but all their songs grow faint; when
men are afraid of heights and of dangers in the streets;
when the almond tree blossoms and the grasshopper
drags himself along and desire no longer is stirred.
Then man goes to his eternal home and mourners go
about the streets. Remember him—before the silver
cord is severed, or the golden bowl is broken; before
the pitcher is shattered at the spring, or the wheel
broken at the well, and the dust returns to the ground
it came from, and the spirit returns to God who gave it
(12:3-7).

Each of these phrases is symbolic of some part of our bodies. "When the keepers of the house tremble" refers to the arms and hands that begin to tremble from feebleness or palsy in old age. "And the strong men stoop" means that our legs become feeble and the knees begin to totter. "When the grinders cease because they are few" is a picture of our teeth, which become fewer in number. "And those looking through the windows grow dim" speaks of the eyes as they weaken and are less able to see, their pupils dilating less and becoming more contracted.

"When the doors to the street are closed" refers to our lips. Because our teeth have fallen out, they are "closed" (a street is an area between two rows of houses). "And the sound of grinding fades" means that since we have so few teeth left, we cannot chew very well and need to trade in our Wheaties for oatmeal! "When men rise up at the sound of birds" means that even the least amount of noise wakens you in the morning and you cannot get back to sleep. "But all their songs grow faint" declares that our hearing lessens and our ability to make and enjoy music begins to escape us.

"When men are afraid of heights" is a reference to the growing fear of falling, "and of dangers in the streets" means that we begin to fear being jostled and injured as we move more slowly and unsteadily. "When the almond tree blossoms" refers to the hair turning white, and "the grasshopper drags himself along" alludes to the halting walk of the elderly as they go on their way. "And desire no longer is stirred" suggests that both sexual desire and power are lost. "Then man goes to his eternal home, and mourners go about the streets" warns of one's impending death and the mourning that will accompany the funeral.

"Remember him—before the silver cord is severed, or the golden bowl is broken" could refer to the spinal cord and the brain; or it could refer to the fragile quality of life (much like a beautiful, golden lamp bowl suspended by a fine silver chain), which can be ended with a snap. The pitcher "shattered at the spring" is a figure of speech for the heart, and "the wheel broken at the well" speaks of the veins and arteries that carry the blood throughout the body like a water wheel.

"And the dust returns to the ground it came from" reminds us of God's words to Adam: "For dust you are, and to dust you will return" (Gen. 3:19). The spirit's returning "to God who gave it" reminds us of the source of our life (see Gen. 2:7).

Solomon says, "Now, before these things happen—and you can be sure that at least some of them will—live for the Lord. Give Him the strength of your strongest days. Use them for God. Don't just give Him what little is left over after you have wasted your strength."

Old age is a marvelous experience of its own, and I do not believe Solomon intends to ridicule it with his vivid word pictures. When a person has lived for God all his or her days, old age can be a glorious time; but it will not be a time of strenuous service for God.

So if we are going to serve the Lord, we must do what we can while we can!

Questions for Discussion

1. What are some of the "million questions" you would like God to answer? What do you suppose His answers might be?
2. What about life today delights you? Why? What causes you concern? Why?
3. Why is it important for a teenager to live for God? What about a college graduate? A newlywed couple? A young mother or father? A middle-aged person? A senior citizen?
4. Are you giving the Lord the strength of your strongest days? What is keeping you from doing so?
5. How would a "50 years from now" perspective affect the way you now live?

CHAPTER TWELVE

The End of All Vanity: God

Ecclesiastes 12:8-14

The experiment is over.

Solomon has ended—as he began—with "meaninglessness." Emptiness. Vanity. He has forced his secular friend to ask the tough questions of life "under the sun." His friend has now faced the harsh realities of life if he is going to be consistently empirical. For all he knows—all he can see, hear, taste, smell, or touch—life without God is a disaster.

The honest person must now ask what he intends to do about what he has learned. Does he really want answers to the questions he has been willing to ask? Is he willing to look at his own life in light of those answers. Or was it just an entertaining exercise of the mind?

Would a sure answer spoil everything?

In *The Great Divorce*, C. S. Lewis constructed an elaborate scenario in which the searcher is being invited into heaven. He is informed by a heavenly being, "'I can promise you . . . no scope for your talents: only forgiveness for having perverted them. No atmosphere of inquiry, for I will bring you to the land not of questions but of answers, and you shall see the face of God.'

"'Ah, but we must all interpret those beautiful words in our own way! For me there is no such thing as *a* final answer. The free wind of inquiry must always continue to blow through the mind, must it not? . . . '

"'Listen!' said the White Spirit. 'Once you were a child. Once you knew what inquiry was for. There was a time when you asked questions because you wanted answers, and were glad when you had found them. Become that child again: even now.'

"'Ah, but when I became a man I put away childish things.'"[1]

Sadly enough, the searcher is content with this state of affairs, and he wanders off to his next appointment. It all made for an interesting discussion for him, but he never realized that the real issues were heaven and hell.

These are the issues with which we have been wrestling, too. What will we do about Solomon's search, and ours?

Fear God and Keep His Commandments

"Meaningless! Meaningless!" says the Teacher.
"Everything is meaningless!" Not only was the
Teacher wise, but also he imparted knowledge to the
people. He pondered and searched out and set in
order many proverbs. The Teacher searched to find
just the right words, and what he wrote was upright
and true. The words of the wise are like goads, their
collected sayings like firmly embedded nails—given by
one Shepherd. Be warned, my son, of anything in
addition to them. Of making many books there is no
end, and much study wearies the body (Eccles. 12:8-
12).

Again the Preacher returns to this thesis: "Everything is meaningless!" One could argue for including verse 8 in the previous section, but I have included it here because it serves as a reminder of Solomon's verdict on all the areas in which humans strive. In the end, all human effort is worthless, futile. It is only in that context, then, that we are ready to hear Solomon's conclusion.

In calling himself wise, Solomon was referring to the three

great religious institutions of his day—the prophets, the priests, and the wise men. He was not being egotistical. A "wise man" was designated as such in recognition of God's gifting him with wisdom, much as we ordain ministers in recognition of God's calling them to ministry.

These sayings serve two purposes. Two images illustrate them—

> Now all has been heard; here is the conclusion of the
> matter: Fear God and keep his commandments, for
> this is the whole duty of man. For God will bring every
> deed into judgment, including every hidden thing,
> whether it is good or evil (12:13, 14).

In contrast to the meaninglessness, or "vanity," that has permeated Ecclesiastes, we are finally presented with that which is not vain: "Fear God and keep his commandments." When we fear God, it puts us into a proper relationship with Him. It is not so much a matter of fear in the sense of terror as it is of fear in the sense of awe. To fear God is to hold Him in awe, to reverence Him. It puts Him in His proper place and reminds us of where we should place all the other elements of our lives—love, joy, sadness, success, failure. If we do so, it will affect everything we do or think. It will cause us to understand and accept our proper place in the universe and will keep us from thinking more highly of ourselves than we should. Only in this way can we escape the folly of the secularist who says, "There is no God" (Ps. 14:1).

When we keep God's commandments, we live consistently with what God has made us to be. I think we often confuse keeping God's commandments with legalism, obeying a list of rules that tell us what we can and cannot do. Instead, we ought to view it as following the plan God mapped out for us in all His magnificent love. He knows what we need; He created us. He loves us, and His commandments are for our good. "Oh, how I love your law!" (Ps. 119:97).

It is comforting to know that "God will bring every deed into judgment" (12:14). If God is concerned enough about me to pass judgment on my life, then ultimately everything in it has value. None of it is vain, or meaningless.

This is the catch. Wise man that he is, Solomon has painted us into a corner. All along he has teased us—and especially those who ignore the Lord—with the fear that nothing has any value, that nothing has any meaning whatsoever. The secularist has had to go along with Solomon's argument. What basis would he have for arguing with him?

Now, here, finally—at "the conclusion of the matter"—Solomon proclaims the truth: God *is* going to pass judgment on our lives. This means that everything is vitally important. Nothing in my life goes unnoticed, much less all of it!

It is a marvelous, joyous, and wonderful truth. The Creator and King of all creation takes us very seriously.

Ultimately, then, the meaning of life turns on this very question. Is it for nothing? Or is it of priceless value?

Solomon has given his answer. You will give yours by the choices you make.

> When the perishable has been clothed with the imperishable, and the mortal with immortality, then the saying that is written will come true: "Death has been swallowed up in victory." Therefore, my dear brothers, stand firm. Let nothing move you. Always give yourselves fully to the work of the Lord, because you know that your labor in the Lord is not in vain (1 Cor. 15:54,58).

> O God, the strength of all them that put their trust in Thee, mercifully accept our prayers; and because through the weaknesses of our mortal nature we can do no good thing without Thee, grant us the help of Thy grace, that in keeping of Thy commandments we may please Thee, both in will and deed, through Jesus Christ our Lord. Amen."[2]

Note
1. C. S. Lewis, *The Great Divorce* (New York, NY: Macmillan, 1946), pp. 40-41.
2. *The Book of Common Prayer* (Oxford: Oxford University Press, 1928), Collect, First Sunday after Trinity.

Questions for Discussion

1. As you view life, is there such a thing as one final answer to your questioning? If not why not? If so, what is that answer?
2. Do you agree with Solomon's final conclusion—that fearing God and keeping His commandments gives life ultimate meaning? Why? Why not?
3. How does Solomon's pronouncement that God will judge every deed make you feel? How should this truth affect the way Christians conduct their lives?
4. What is your answer to Solomon's key question? Is life meaningless, or does it have meaning? What is the real value of life?

More Bible Commentaries for Laymen from Regal Books

Confronted by Love: God's Principles for Daily Living from 2 Corinthians—Dan Baumann. This study vividly speaks about God's will, evangelism, victory in Christ and other subjects for today's Christian. S391101
Teacher's Manual **AB615**

God with Us: Themes from Matthew—D.A. Carson. This thorough and practical study provides an overview of the themes which contribute to this Gospel's widespread popularity. S392106   Teacher's Manual **AB625**

God's Way Out: Finding the Road to Personal Freedom Through Exodus—Bernard Ramm. Exodus is more than the saga of God leading His people out of bondage. It is a look at divine redemption showing God's way out of slavery to the world. S416154   Teacher's Manual **AB955**

Let's Keep Growing: Encouragement from 1 and 2 Thessalonians—Harold Fickett. Today's Christians will find reassurance and answers to such questions as how we can please God and what we can expect when Christ returns to earth. S415146   Teacher's Manual **AB935**

Winning the Battles of Life: A Life-Related Study of Joshua—Paul E. Toms. The theme of conquest in Joshua reminds believers that God has the power to lead us into victory in each daily conflict. S413129
Teacher's Manual **AB915**

**Look for these and other Regal titles
at your regular Christian bookstore.**